CONTEMPORARY ISSUES
IN CRIMINAL JUSTICE

CONTEMPORARY ISSUES IN CRIMINAL JUSTICE

Some Problems and Suggested Reforms

Edited by

RUDOLPH J. GERBER

National University Publications
KENNIKAT PRESS / 1976
Port Washington, N. Y. / London

Manufactured in the United States of America

Published by
Kennikat Press Corp.
Port Washington, N.Y./London

Library of Congress Cataloging in Publication Data
Main entry under title:

Contemporary issues in criminal justice.

(National university publications)
Many of these ideas were first presented at a
national symposium in criminal law at Arizona State
University in 1974, under the auspices of the Law
Enforcement Assistance Administration.

1. Criminal justice, Administration of—United
States—Addresses, essays, lectures. I. Gerber,
Rudolph J. II. Arizona. State University, Tempe.
III. United States. Law Enforcement Assistance
Administration.
KF9223.A75C66   364   75-37507
ISBN 0-8046-9115-0

CONTENTS

PREFACE

It comes as no shock to the well-informed that this nation's criminal justice system is on the verge of collapse. Indeed, five years ago authoritative presidential commissions were sounding the same warning, but an aura of disbelief surrounded the ad-monitors themselves at the time. These last five years have made believers of us all. FBI crime indexes rise in volume each year with a regularity that would be the envy of the stock market. Warehoused ex-cons return to their warehouses for recycling at the same determined rate as they are released. These ware-houses now resemble graduate schools of crime, with a pedigreed list of continuing education courses to transform the novice into the professional. Last and seemingly least, the forgotten average citizen bereft of his stereo, automobile, peace of mind—possibly of life or limb as well—needs hardly to be told that the law enforcement system in his community has collapsed. All he cares to know is that the glut of crime needs a glut of new ideas to restore some semblance of order to the criminal justice system before we revert to vigilante groups, armed camps, and cavemen.

This book contains some mature, well-rehearsed proposals for hope and for change in the system. The contributors, all recognized authorities in diverse fields of criminal law and jus-tice, have given long thought to what eats at the present system and what would be most able to restore its failing powers to do its task of crime control. Many of these ideas were first presented at a national symposium in criminal law at Arizona State Univer-sity in 1974, under the generous auspices of the Law Enforcement Assistance Administration, partly to inaugurate that University's

Criminal Justice Center and headquarters for the National Criminal Justice Consortium, and partly to stimulate substantive revision of criminal law. The ideas presented then and elsewhere and subsequently collected here represent careful analysis of present law enforcement deficiencies and practical suggestions on how to go about it better.

Part One addresses areas of legislative reform. In chapter one, Professor Skolnick suggests that private, consensual sex be off-limits for criminal law. Michael Shagan, who helps run this country's largest legal lottery, next points out a similar horizon for gambling: ill-enforced, archaic laws reflecting the morality of yesterday stand in the way of more legal and more lucrative sources of finances for hard-pressed state treasuries. Obscenity needs a new approach too, according to Dr. Gerber; its enforcement resembles a checkerboard in the wake of recent Supreme Court decisions, so now there is need for a middle ground between outright condemnation and outright legalization.

In Part Two, addressed to problems of court administration, our arthritic jury system, substantially unchanged since the Norman Conquest, evokes a plea for professional upgrading from Dr. Shuman and John Mowen. Professor McAnany makes a plea to improve probation services and criticizes the official notion that probation be subsumed into—and submerged by—a statewide correctional administration. Perhaps the foremost authority on crime compensation, Professor Gilbert Geis, next provides the reasons for compensating innocent victims of violent crime; he adds an analysis of the merits of the few state programs already operating.

In Part Three, dealing with correctional reform, David Fogel, the former innovative Corrections Commissioner in Minnesota, contrasts the fortress prison with the justice model and suggests what a prison should be—not a warehouse but a laboratory of justice. Professor Norval Morris and Michael Mills next consider one of the most controversial aspects of contemporary prison life — volunteering for often dangerous medical experiments—and suggest reforms to secure the advantages of more careful experimentation.

Finally, in Part Four, addressed to innovative minds wherever they may be hiding, within or without the crime control system, Gerald Caplan offers an administrator's summary of crucial areas of on-going research likely to better the performance of witnesses, victims, police, courts, and corrections.

The contributors would not risk their reputations on the promise that their recommendations will inter the crime problem once and for all. Their humble hope, however, is to have helped turn one of the first spades in that direction.

R. J. Gerber

Phoenix, Arizona

CONTEMPORARY ISSUES IN CRIMINAL JUSTICE

I

ENFORCEMENT PRIORITIES FOR LEGISLATURES AND LAWMEN

JEROME H. SKOLNICK

1. SHOULD SEXUAL RELATIONS BE TREATED AS CRIMES?

The issue of what the *law* ought to do about sex is rather different from what *we* ought to do about it. People ought to enjoy as much and as diverse sexual activity as they find pleasurable, while the legal system should engage in a policy of total sexual abstinence, i.e., should not punish on the basis of sexual aspects of conduct alone. I am thus not talking about forcible sex, involving assaults on the human body, or sex involving children. I am talking about voluntary sex, between or among consenting adults.

The flaws arising from enforcement of consenting adult sex have become particularly prominent during the past decade, in the framework of a shift in sexual morality from public puritanism to public diversity. Let me elaborate.

Sexual Revolution?

Whether or not there has been a sexual revolution in the last decade or so, there has surely been a serious questioning among large segments of the population of traditional sex norms. We live in a contemporary world of diversity rather than unanimity. Accordingly, attempts to impose restraints on private consensual sexual activities cannot conform to the opinions of an overwhelming majority, and therefore will be difficult to enforce. When sex laws are enforced, they must be enforced unfairly.

Jerome H. Skolnick is Chairman of the Center for Study of Law and Society and Professor of Criminology, University of California, Berkeley.

First, let me give some evidence for changing sexual norms. In 1970, my wife and I edited a book which we were to call *Family in Transition.*[1] We gave it that title because while gathering material for the volume we came across such items in newspapers and magazines as the following:

1. A feature newspaper article about the effects of longevity on marriage, questioning whether twenty-year-olds can realistically make marriage contracts that will remain emotionally valid fifty years hence.

2. An editorial in a prestigious science journal urging that the population explosion makes parenthood a privilege rather than a right, and that women must be educated to seek careers other than multiple motherhood. If such inducements as community child-care facilities and state rewards for not having children fail to reduce the birth rate, the author suggests that women be sterilized.

3. An article in the Parent and Child Department of the *New York Times* Sunday Magazine listing thirteen wrong reasons for having children, including the desire for immortality and the couples' parents' desires for grandchildren. Instead, the prospective grandparents are advised to find fulfillment in a more active sex life. The article asserts that childrearing is so demanding of time, effort, and talent that very few can really be good at it, especially people who are ambitious in their work.

4. An article in the Sunday Entertainment Section of a newspaper on a large number of movies about troubled marriage. By now it is almost a Hollywood cliché to portray marriage as unhappy, particularly when the partners are middle-aged and affluent.

5. A series of articles in a major West Coast newspaper on homosexuals as a minority group. In the article, male and female homosexuals present the case for viewing homosexuality as a valid way of life. Included in this way of life are homosexual marriages and the bringing up of children.

A content analysis of the mass media during the past few years would reveal other challenges to conventional views on sex, marriage, and family, such as communal living and women's liberation. Not only have restrictions on sexual themes in movies, books, and stage plays been dramatically loosened, but whole industries have grown up around the theme of women's liberation and new moralities concerning marriage and sexual life.

Some writers have argued that marriage is no less an imposing social institution than it used to be. Despite rising divorce rates, more people are getting married more times than ever. In other words, there are fewer people who never marry and more multiple marriages. Thus, it is argued, marriage is even more important than it ever was, because people are trying very hard to find compatible mates rather than remain with unsatisfactory ones. But the argument misses the point about marriage as a normative institution. It has lost its taken-for-granted lifelong quality.

In a sense, the Roman Catholic view of marriage had a kind of emotional if not doctrinal validity for most people until recently. This is what has changed. The possibility of divorce is an unspoken but significant part of marriage vows today. As one writer has suggested, both partners remain permanently available on the marriage market until death do them part. Thus the ground rules of marriage have changed so much that one finds articles in women's magazines warning against getting divorced too easily. One author, a marriage counselor, wrote of a number of instances of arguments escalating into divorce threats and even into actual divorce, without either partner really wanting to go that far. The main point about marriage now is that it seems to possess an unprecedented fragility, no matter how many times people marry and remarry.

Similarly, I have heard it argued that a sexual revolution is not taking place because behavior has not really changed all that much since the 1920s—it is just that people have become more open about their behavior. There are two difficulties with this argument. First, it often assumes that projections of the future are soundly made on the basis of prior regularities. For example, several writers have argued that Kinsey found little change in the behavior among women born in 1920 to 1929, compared to their mothers. On the basis of that finding, it is assumed that regularities will continue for girls born from 1945 to 1955. Second, even if behavior were to remain the same and only attitudes changed, that would be extraordinary in itself. Hypocrisy, La Rochefoucauld noted, is the homage that vice renders to virtue. Previous generations of secret swingers connived in upholding the puritanical definitions of morality.

Let me say further that arguments back and forth about numbers—about how many young women are having intercourse with how many men before they are married, about how many affairs there are, about how many homosexuals there are—all of these arguments obscure a vital point, namely, that behavior is a form of communication where the same act can have different meanings according to its moral context. For example, an unmarried girl's affair with a man may be seen by her and others in a context of sin and remorse, as in the old-fashioned confession magazine stories. That sort of confession or expression of so-called deviance serves to reinforce conventional morality. Alternatively, those violating conventional norms may not actually adhere to conventional standards but still respect them outwardly by keeping variant behavior discreet. This second approach undermines conventional morality but does not really challenge it. The third alternative is to defy conventional standards openly, as happens when young men and women live openly together without being married, when unwed movie actresses publicize their pregnancies, when homosexuals picket in support of gay liberation, or when women's liberation denounces marriage and advocates masturbation.

Whether or not this defiance is accepted, the open violation of conventional norms and the publicity lavished on famous violators by the media must affect even the most conservative elements of society. As William Graham Sumner pointed out long ago, much of the force of moral rules rests in their being taken for granted, in the unthinkability of their being questioned, and the assumption, sometimes unconscious, that terrible consequences will follow upon their violation. The failure of public sinners to suffer either guilt or the wrath of God further undermines the authority of the moral rule. Indeed, once a moral rule becomes the subject of debate, no matter how the debate comes out, it can scarcely maintain its sacred character. The more sexual norms are discussed, the more sexual diversity becomes acceptable and the more life becomes both eroticized and politicized.

Although the open flaunting of unconventional behavior in the name of alternative standards is perhaps the most dramatically different feature of the present times, social change may occur even in the absence of large numbers of new recruits to the ranks of the so-called "deviants." As Gagnon and Simon comment:

. . . significant social change does not come about only when there have been changes in overt behavior patterns. The moment of change may simply be the point at which new forms of behavior appear possible. An example of this phenomenon of the increased plausibility of a behavior without behavioral change is the current status of homosexuality as a public topic. There is no evidence that there has been a growth in the proportion of the population with homosexual preferences. . . . [The homosexual] still faces the risk of arrest, conviction, or imprisonment, and the more frequent costs of rejection by friends, family, or loss of employment.

Nevertheless, in recent years homosexuality has become one of the standard fares on the frontiers of the American cultural scene. . . .[2]

The notion of plausibility suggests that whether or not there has been revolutionary change in familial sex and childrearing behavior, such change now appears possible to increasingly large numbers of people, perhaps especially to young people.

Cultural Lag in the Courts

What we encounter today, then, is a marked revision, if not a revolution in conceptions of sexual morality. Eventually, the law—both legislatures and courts—will catch up with changes in morality, but the law will likely always lag behind. Sometimes the courts will do what legislatures fear to do, as the United States Supreme Court did in the recent abortion cases. But recall the enormous effort required of those in Connecticut to receive the approval of the United States Supreme Court for operating a

Planned Parenthood clinic in New Haven, Connecticut. One wonders about the law's capacity to catch up with social change.

A more recent example: In California, a state that is both in conflict and in transition over the law's role in sexual morality, the Supreme Court recently handed down a decision that exemplifies everything that is wrong with the whole business of the law trying to enforce private sexual morality. The case is Pettit v. State Board of Education decided on September 7, 1973 (109 Cal. Rptr. 665). In the case the court is asked to review a judgment denying the plaintiff mandate to vacate an order of the State Board of Education revoking her elementary school life diploma on the grounds that she engaged in certain acts of sexual misconduct evidencing her unfitness to teach. The court concludes that the conduct furnishes ample ground to support the order of revocation. The facts are these: for thirteen years the plaintiff taught mentally retarded elementary school children, a task that requires exceptional skill and patience. Her competence throughout her career was unquestioned. Not a scintilla of evidence ever suggested that she in any way failed properly to perform her professional responsibilities. But in November 1967, after a ten-year career of teaching, the plaintiff, then forty-eight years old, and her husband applied for membership in a club called "The Swingers." This was a private club in Los Angeles whose main purpose was to provide a facility for various sexual activities between members at club parties. The club was advertised in a Los Angeles underground newspaper. Membership was open to single men and women and to couples, who were required to show a health certificate certifying they were free of venereal disease. Females were admitted to the club free of charge, while males were required to pay an initiation fee of $25.00 and a monthly fee of $5.00. There seemed to be more interest by single males than single females, and the former were accordingly discouraged from joining. Mainly, the club membership consisted of couples.

A Sergeant Berk, who worked as an undercover agent for the Los Angeles Police Department, clandestinely joined the club —allegedly on the anonymous complaint of a female who had sought membership—in order to investigate it. On December 2,

1967, he attended a party at a private residence during which he said he saw numerous sexual activities, including various couples engaged in sexual intercourse. According to Sergeant Berk, both bedrooms of the house where the club was located were in almost constant use by various couples engaging in acts of sexual intercourse. People were walking in and out of the bedrooms, watching the couples in the beds engaging in various sex acts. Both males and females were walking around the house in various stages of undress to nudity. Berk testified that he saw the plaintiff commit three separate acts of oral copulation with three different men at the party, and that when these acts took place the participants were undressed and other persons were looking on.

The plaintiff was subsequently arrested and charged with violating California Penal Code Sec. 288A (oral copulation). A plea bargain was evidently arranged and the plaintiff pleaded guilty to Penal Code Sec. 650.5 (outraging public decency), which is a misdemeanor. A fine was imposed and the plaintiff was placed on probation. Upon payment of the fine probation was terminated and the criminal proceedings were dismissed.

In February 1970, for reasons undisclosed in the Supreme Court opinion, disciplinary proceedings were initiated to revoke the plaintiff's teaching credentials on the grounds, among others, that her conduct involved moral turpitude and demonstrated her unfitness to teach. A board hearing was held where Sergeant Berk testified as summarized above. Her husband, Mr. Pettit, also testified. He said that the plaintiff had realized in advance sexual activities would occur at the swingers club party, and that with her consent he had observed her engage in sexual intercourse and oral copulation with other men in the past.

Moreover, he and Mrs. Pettit had appeared on the Joe Pyne Television Show in 1966 and on another similar show, and they had on both occasions discussed nonconventional sexual life styles. Subjects such as adultery and wife-swapping were discussed and the Pettits had expressed the philosophical attitude of not being "up tight" about these matters. In the course of the TV discussions the couple wore masks and Mr. Pettit a false beard as well so that they were not able to be observed.

At the board hearing, a psychiatrist testified on behalf of the plaintiff that she was well adjusted except for the trauma and emotional turmoil caused by her suspension. Her school principal introduced an evaluation saying that her teaching was quite satisfactory and indeed there was a contract of employment with her school district offering to rehire her for the 1968/69 school year. Three school superintendents testified that she was unfit to teach on grounds that a teacher must set a good moral example for pupils and that she might inject her ideas regarding sexual morals into the classroom. Although there was no evidence that this had happened, the hearing examiner concluded that the plaintiff's act did constitute moral turpitude and evidenced her unfitness for service. It was concluded that her life diploma ought to be revoked. A majority of the Supreme Court upheld the hearing examiner, Justice Burke writing for the majority.

There was a dissent, written by Justice Tobriner and joined in by Justice Mosk, two paragraphs of which I think adequately summarize the whole problem of the attempt of the state to regulate private consensual sex.

In the instant case the conduct involved consensual sexual behavior which deviated from traditional norms. Yet recognized authority tells us the practice pursued here is, indeed, quite common. An estimated '95% of adult American men and a large percentage of American women have experienced orgasm in an illegal manner.' (McCary, *Human Sexuality* (2nd ed. 1973) p. 460.) The 1953 Kinsey report, *Sexual Behavior in the Human Female,* at page 399 indicates that 62% of the adult women of plaintiff's educational level and age range engage in oral copulation; more recently, the report's co-authors have stated that newer studies suggest the figure now lies around 75 to 80 percent.

The consensual and, as I shall explain, private act did not affect, and could not have affected, plaintiff's teaching ability. The whole matter would have been forgotten and lost in the limbo of the privacy of its occurrence if it had not been clandestinely observed by means of a surreptitious intrusion which reminds one of the surveillance of restrooms which this court has condemned. (People v. Triggs 1973, 8 Cal.3d 884, 106 Cal. Rptr. 408, 506 P.2d 232.) The commission of a sex act, surreptitiously observed, not disclosed to fellow teachers or to pupils, not remotely adversely affecting plaintiff's teaching ability, must fail to support revocation of the certificate even though the act is labelled 'criminal' on the books.

This case adequately reveals fundamental problems arising out of the attempt to prescribe private consensual sexual conduct by attaching criminal penalties to deviations therefrom.

First, as times change, the law invites hypocrisy. There may indeed be a person in this distinguished assemblage who has failed to commit a sex crime, but why should such a strange creature—statistically strange, that is—serve as a legal model for us all?

Joking aside, since so-called unconventional sex acts are not really so unconventional anyhow, enforcement cannot only not be even-handed, but must be capricious. This private club of swingers somehow came to the attention of the police. Others exist throughout California. So long as they exist in private, who cares? The anonymous complainant in this case need not have answered a newspaper ad, nor need she have read the underground newspaper. Indeed, the swingers' proprietor at least showed a concern for public health by requiring a V.D. certificate as a condition of membership. Such a requirement hardly prevails at numerous "singles" bars and other places facilitating sexual alliances.

Besides, the police and courts are overworked, understaffed, and overcrowded. The enforcement of private, consensual sex crimes uses resources better spent to protect the safety of streets and other public places and residences. Really, didn't the L.A.P.D. have something better to do with Sergeant Berk's time? Should taxpayers bear the burden of voyeuristic law enforcement? As Justice Tobriner commented, the woman took reasonable precautions to assure that she was viewed only by persons who would not be offended by her conduct. Many would argue that under such circumstances her behavior was neither imprudent nor immoral.

Besides, although the direct penalties for sex crime enforcement may be trivial, formal conviction, even of a misdemeanor, need not lead merely to a small fine, but may, as in the Pettit case, result in loss of job and substantial earnings.

Finally, the convicted defendant in a private, consensual sex crime case is not the only loser. So also is the community a loser when the defendant is a competent person, and particularly a competent professional person. One can hardly improve upon

Justice Tobriner's dissenting conclusion in the Pettit case, when he states: "In conclusion, I submit that the majority opinion is blind to the reality of sexual behavior. Its views that teachers in their private lives should exemplify Victorian principles of sexual morality, and in the classroom should subliminally indoctrinate the pupils in such principles, is hopelessly unrealistic and atavistic. The children of California are entitled to competent and dedicated teachers; when, as in this case, such a teacher is forced to abandon her lifetime profession, the children are the losers."

Unacceptable Costs

One can hardly improve upon this conclusion, but it is perhaps worthwhile to add the following: As sexual behavior and sexual morality change, the costs of law enforcement must increase beyond anything acceptable to the general community. Ultimately, the overburdened taxpayer must bear the cost of a fruitless attempt to use public funds to enforce private and increasingly questioned conceptions of morality. An eighteenth-century puritanical legislator who believed strongly in premarital chastity might have considered it wise to enact laws forbidding fornication. Before the Revolution—the American one—it was considered the proper province of the law to enforce the will of God. Fornication was accordingly enacted into law as a major crime. But those laws were no more honored, and no less capriciously enforced, than contemporary statutes attempting to govern the private consensual sex behavior of adults. As historian David H. Flaherty concludes on the basis of his studies of law and morals in early America:

Practically every scholar who has studied this subject has commented on the existence of widespread sexual irregularities. A random examination of county court records in any of the New England colonies would illustrate this situation. New England legal machinery prosecuted many breaches of the moral laws, but the violations remained numerous. Legislative repression of sexual misbehavior did not succeed, despite the continued experiments with types of laws and punishments. . . . [3]

As we look toward the twenty-first century, it is time finally to comprehend that where sexual conduct is private, it is not the law's business. Such statutes can only encourage law enforcement processes that are so impractical, so arbitrary, and so needlessly costly as surely to diminish respect for law as a rational and legitimate model for defining and resolving complex social issues.

NOTES

1. Arlene Skolnick and Jerome H. Skolnick, *Family in Transition* (Boston: Little, Brown & Co., 1971).
2. John H. Gagnon and William Simon, *The Sexual Scene* (Chicago: Aldine Publishing Company, 1970), pp. 10–12.
3. David H. Flaherty, "Law and the Enforcement of Morals in Early America." *Perspectives in American History 5* (Cambridge: Harvard University Press, 1971), pp. 225–26.

MICHAEL D. SHAGAN

2. IS GAMBLING WORTH ENFORCEMENT GAMBLE?

By way of initiation, here are some personal, critical views about criminal law and its relation to gambling.

First, it is counter-productive for there to be gambling statutes which go far beyond the limits of effective law enforcement. Effective law enforcement should be viewed not only in terms of what enforcement can accomplish through the criminal justice system, but what enforcement is acceptable by the people as appropriate. For instance: The Illinois Gambling Statute makes no distinction between commercial gambling and social gambling. But when Chicago Police arrested a group of prominent citizens who were playing a friendly game of poker, the superintendent of police announced on the front pages that he was sorry; his policy he said was *not* to arrest for gambling in the absence of a commercial element.

This distinction, based on whether the gambling act involves a commercial element rather than merely equal participants, is a reasonable one to draw. Social gambling which does not contain this extra element should *not* be held a violation of law.

Secondly, the concept of violations of gambling laws as "victimless crimes" is useful, but a word of caution: It is certainly true that "a gambler may look like an innocent offender when compared to a murderer or a rapist; however, the gambler is the nexus of the power and influence of organized crime."[1] Helping to "finance" an illegal gambling operation ends up helping to finance loan sharking, drug pushing, the invasion of legitimate

Michael D. Shagan is Vice-President of the New York City Off-Track Betting Corporation.

businesses through strong-arm or other tactics, and so forth. So in a real sense, our whole society can be thought of as the "victim" of illegal gambling. But it is difficult to convey this point to the illegal bettor, especially when he has no alternative outlet for his betting interests, and when he sees the corner bookmaker either not arrested at all; or if arrested, almost always merely slapped on the wrist by a fine or other light penalty in a way which has been described as the illegal gambling fraternity's "license [fee] to engage in gambling."

In 1970, the New York City Police Department spent over 7 million dollars in manpower costs to investigate gambling offenses (not including the costs of equipment, court processing, and prosecution of gambling offenses). Of the 2,519 felony arrests made that year, only 25 resulted in felony convictions, none of which resulted in spent time in a state prison. For the six years of 1965 through 1970, 19,491 felony arrests were made, 1,499 indictments were handed down; there were a total of 93 felony convictions, 42 fines were levied, 21 local jail sentences resulted, and but one individual was sentenced to a state prison for his felony. While the volume of these figures is of a different proportion in New York than elsewhere, the experience is hardly dissimilar elsewhere.

The adverse effect of this disturbing record of law enforcement is not merely in the success of the illegal gambling activity: rather it is compounded by the incredible amount of resources deferred from the policing and prosecution of other crimes, including crimes of violence; and the loss of faith by the public in government, in the law, and in the public office holders involved in the functioning of government and the law. There is also the failure of morale within the police, who find themselves in the unenviable position of being law enforcers who are not really expected to enforce the gambling laws. For the honest policeman assigned to gambling enforcement units, only professional frustration can result. For the corruptible policeman, prosecutor, or judge, the ability to rationalize an opportunity for personal gain becomes significant.

The study by the Hudson Institute points out that stringent enforcement of gambling laws, and especially tough sentencing, would in many ways increase substantially the bookmaker's cost of doing business. The study goes on to point out, however, that for this alone to be a satisfactory means of dealing with the problem, 2 to 4 million dollars would have to be expended yearly for the additional administrative burden of handling the increased caseload. This portion of the study concludes:

Since New York City is now sending less than 600 men a year to prison (for felonies) after trial, it would *not* be a reasonable use of criminal justice system resources to try to put 100 bookies a year in jail. There would not be much use in putting only a few in jail, unless it were possible to get the principal operators.

In effect, the criminal law is *not* available as a tool to carry out a policy against gambling. The system has broken down completely.

As a result of this dilemma, in the fall of 1971, the New York City Police Department reorganized and downgraded its efforts in the area of gambling enforcement. It is now concentrating on the quality of gambling arrests (the principal operators) and is leaving the street corner bookie alone, unless he can be tied back to his higher-ups. This has allowed some two-thirds of the gambling squad to be transferred over to narcotics enforcement duty or to the prevention of violent street crime. Another major impetus for this move was the findings of the "Knapp Commission" about police corruption in New York: it was agreed that an official policy against arresting individual bookies will keep such bookies from making pay-offs to police officers, because they no longer have to fear arrests by these policemen.

The police department policy, while logical and understandable, unfortunately may tend to induce more illegal gambling. As reported in the *New York Daily News* on October 31, 1973, numbers operators say that graft costs have gone way down, and consequently profits are higher then ever.

The additional unfortunate aspect of this situation is that the Police Department change in approach occurred at just the same time the Off-Track Betting Corporation (OTB) was reaching maturity in New York. Thus, while OTB may have greatly reduced unlawful betting on horseracing, it is by no means certain that the result, to this point, has been a net decrease in all illegal gambling: there could well have been a net increase.

What would appear to be suggested from all of this is that no one tactic will help eliminate illegal gambling, whether it be tough sentencing, more undercover work by the police, wiretapping laws which protect civil liberties but allow law enforcement agencies to function against organized criminal elements, or legalized gambling in competition to the illegal enterprise. All of these are important, but what seems to be needed is a coordinated, broadscale attack on the problem, encompassing all of these ideas, and more, and sustained for three to five years!

Based on the Hudson Institute study and other sources and ideas, here are some possible elements of such a broadscale attack:

1. Competition for customers (i.e., legalization).
2. Advertising, used to pull away customers.
3. Criminal prosecutions vigorously followed through, whenever evidence is available, and especially against middle-level and high-level operatives.
4. End anonymity for the bettor who is found to bet with bookies. In other words, use the fear of embarrassment to get the bettor to switch to the legal alternative.
5. In this same vein, have law enforcement and tax agencies give special attention to those people found to be betting illegally, on the assumption they must have something to hide.
6. Change federal tax laws so as to exempt from the income tax winnings derived from a state-approved legal gambling enterprise. This would take away what is perhaps the bookie's biggest advantage, the ability of his customer to get away more easily in not paying the tax due on winnings.
7. The use of civil remedies against bookmakers, including injunctions, income tax law enforcement, and the enforcement of various areas of state and federal regulatory and tax laws applicable to all businesses including bookmaking. The Hudson Institute suggests hiring civil lawyers to help various agencies in this regard, the salaries of such additional staffing to be recovered by seizures of

cash, fines and civil penalties which result from this effort.

8. Government agencies with responsibility for the licensing of premises where liquor is served, or other similar licensing, should vigorously enforce their right to revoke a license where illegal activity has been permitted on the premises.

9. Consider laws barring the presentation of point-spreads in the Mass Media, a major source of stimulation of sports betting.

10. Finally, here is one example that occurred recently as quoted from the *New York Post* of November 28, 1973:

"A task force of 160 IRS agents and police intelligence officers moved in at dawn today on 86 gamblers believed to be connected with organized crime seizing their cars and placing liens on their homes and other property for failure to pay proper gambling taxes.

The operation was known as "JAB"—Jeopardy Against Bookmakers. . . .

In preparation for the raids, police and IRS agents reviewed for the past eight months gambling records seized by the Public Morals Division on bookmaking and policy arrests to determine the daily volume and profit of each gambler. With those figures as a base, the individual tax bills were computed to determine how much Wagering Excise Tax each owed. It was then found that in all cases the gamblers had failed to pay substantial portions of the taxes due and police then checked into the property each gambler owned that could be seized to satisfy the bill.

'Up until now these guys knew that they were going to get a $250 fine when they were arrested so they always pleaded guilty and paid the fine,' a high police official said. 'The guilty plea was an admission and now they're going to have to pay the tax on it.' "

The Legalization Alternatives

In the 1973 version of the All-American Soap Box Derby, the apparent winner was disqualified because of his use of an electromagnetic device to aid acceleration at the start of the race.

If the sponsors of the race responded to this information by deciding to discontinue such races, this would be a very drastic reaction. Indeed, it is one that was seriously considered. A response far more in keeping with the event would be to make sure it could not happen again, by increased vigilance in the future and by changing certain procedures.

However, were the event in question an adult sporting event, on which bets were legally taken, and a similar kind of fraud had taken place, the cry would not be merely to tighten security, but rather to do away with legal betting on the event, if not with the sport itself.

On the question of gambling, there can hardly be any absolute: all is relative, and depends upon individual perspective and goals. Any endeavor in life involves a gamble, or at least elements of chance or risk. If one decides to invest in corporate stocks, he can choose from many different stocks to buy, depending on how much risk he cares to take. He is free to make that choice, and to gamble with his money by "taking a flyer" on less established securities. Similarly, when a major corporation launches a new product, such as the Edsel, that corporation is clearly risking its investment. It too is "gambling" on consumer acceptance.

But in the two situations postulated, the stock purchase and the new product, a lot more goes into the selection process than mere guesswork. The sponsor of the new product will plan his approach carefully. He will take advantage of the latest techniques in market research and test-marketing. He will establish his growth goals, and produce advertising and other promotional material aimed at achieving these goals. Finally, he will project a financial statement to give him his best estimate of what goals will be accomplishable, or accomplished, for what resources expended. A gamble? Sure it is a gamble, but one where the "odds" can be lowered to manageable proportions through the planning and goal-formulation process which I have indicated.

What about a foray into legalized gambling? It does not have to be a "cold turkey" plunge into a new venture, with no understanding of its economic viability on state revenues, its acceptance by the public, or its other effects. Rather, it should be looked at by policy planners as a new venture just like any other new venture: full of potential pitfalls but equally capable of analysis as is—for instance, a new highway; or a bond issue for a new sports arena; or a program designed to end water pollution; or a projected increase in the sales tax or property tax; or any other program with implications for either government policy, government regulation or control, or questionable public interest or acceptance. You should not go into any of these kinds of ventures without feasibility planning, but likewise you must not be afraid to do the planning. Part of that planning process includes a consideration of all "political factors," such as public acceptance and the likelihood of legislative approval. Thus, once all that planning has been done, you should not be afraid to carry out the logical follow-up to the conclusions of your studies.

My bias, then, is that there is nothing inherent in the concept of legal gambling that should make a person compelled to decide that he must not even consider the issue. In fact, in this day and age, every policy-maker has an ethical duty to carefully consider the questions posed in this short presentation, without rejecting them out-of-hand. Should you gamble on legalized gambling? Legalized gambling may not be right for some particular jurisdictions, but this becomes apparent only once you analyze the hierarchy of goals one reasonably hopes to accomplish through the legalization of gambling compared with the feasibility of accomplishing those goals.

Stated a better way, the question is· what can or cannot be accomplished through legalizing one or more carefully-defined forms of legalized gambling, and do the chances of success in achieving the desired accomplishments outweigh the risks of the experiment?

History

At Common Law, gambling was not a crime, although fraud in connection with gambling would be punishable, and maintaining a gambling operation could have been deemed a public nuisance. The American colonists, therefore, were not acquainted with a history of prohibition of gambling and apparently (with the exception of the Quakers) did not see a heavy moral issue involved.

Aside from local horseracing, and the inevitable wager which accompanied it, the lottery seems to have been the principal general form of gambling in our early period, both Colonial and post-Revolution.[2] In addition to being an accepted form of entertainment, it was socially accepted as a means of seeking revenue. Many lotteries were sanctioned for public benefit, either as a supplemental source of governmental revenues, or because the benefit to be derived might well have been foregone, if additional tax burdens would have been necessary. For example, in North Carolina in 1786, a lottery was granted for the purpose of financing a county poorhouse, it being officially declared "difficult from the variety of taxes now levied on the inhabitants to raise a sufficient sum by a tax."

Other lotteries were for quasi-public purposes, such as the building of colleges. Still others were for the benefit of private persons, such as in the sale, by lottery, of private land or merchandise. Although merchants attempting to sell their merchandise in the usual manner increasingly objected to this use of lotteries, no less a personage than Thomas Jefferson defended this practice.

Here are three interesting examples of lotteries held in Rhode Island in 1762: selling private goods for a Captain, "whose ships had been captured by the enemy and whose partner had gone bankrupt leaving him with the debts"; ransoming a hostage held by the French in the West Indies; and "relieving a jailor who had gone into debt because so many of his prisoners had enlisted in the colonial army and had gone away without paying their board bills."

"Lotteries made an important contribution to colonial finances, providing a means of collecting funds for projects too costly for the local governments, or too large for private parties to handle unaided. . . . The Colonial and Confederation periods set the pattern for lotteries which would be followed with slight deviation for the next 100 years. By 1790 lotteries were so strongly entrenched in the economy and habits of the American people that even if there had been strong opposition, State legislatures only reluctantly would have considered abolishing the schemes. However, opposition was not strong. Most people were willing to pay the cost for a chance to win the munificent prizes."

The next step was the transition of the lottery into a big business. There came into being a class of lottery middlemen known as lottery brokers (professional lottery ticket sellers) and another group known as lottery contractors (professional lottery operators who would utilize the brokers as their agents). One author refers to this emerging system as "the genesis of American big business, for many of the promotional and organizational techniques originated by these groups later were used to advantage by all types of business concerns."

These early manual lottery systems were fraught with possibilities for fraud. With the advent of a class of professional lotterymen, the public exposure of the abuses which took place was greatly increased. In addition, state restrictions on the sale of lottery tickets from other states were often flagrantly ignored. Organized opposition began to develop, not led by the churches although often joined by the churches once public opinion had developed some anti-lottery momentum.

At first, the response by state governments was the tightening of regulations, but the movement for outright abolition persisted. As of 1840, lotteries were prohibited in twelve states; by the Civil War, all but three states had such prohibitions. While there was a resurgence of lotteries after the Civil War, well-publicized abuses of lotteries—especially the national attention focused on the infamous Louisiana Lottery—finally resulted in successful congressional action in 1895, prohibiting the use by lottery companies of interstate commerce in any form for the transportation of lottery material. At the start of the twentieth century, thirty-six state constitutions prohibited lotteries. Even today, Nevada's Constitution still contains a ban on lotteries.

Lottery drawings stretched over a number of days. The methodology involved drawing a number and matching it with a second drawing which would be either a winning "prize" or a losing "blank." Numerous side-bets and other financial practices developed out of this methodology. One such betting practice was available to those who wished to wager even less than the price of the lottery ticket: The bettor would bet on whether a particular number would be drawn at all (whether or not a winner), during a particular period of time, and the bettor's receipt for this kind of wager was known as an "insurance policy" or "policy." Note that in this unauthorized outgrowth of even legal lotteries, all proceeds would go to the lottery brokers, and none went as taxes or other revenues to the intended beneficiary of the legal lottery. Even after lotteries were prohibited, this "policy" game continued, with the brokers merely coming up with some other determinant of the winning number. The present-day, illegal "policy game" or "numbers game" is a direct descendant of this early practice.

Present Gambling Variations

Illegal gambling in the United States today takes on a number of different forms. Using New York State as an example, there does not appear to be any major problem with illegal casino gambling. Bookmaking consists of horse betting and sports betting, the latter being heavy on football, basketball, and baseball. There is also the "Sports Pool Card," where the bettor sets up a parlay in which he predicts the outcome of three or more sporting events. And, of course, there is the Numbers Game.

Sources of information on the scope and volume of illegal gambling are obviously limited, but the following figures may be useful to give a rough idea of what we are contending with.

1. A study by the Hudson Institute in January 1973 estimated that New Yorkers gamble in excess of 4 billion dollars a year (excluding private betting). Of this total, the study estimates 2.1 billion was bet legally (at racetracks, and with off-track betting, the State lottery, and bingo), and that an additional 1.85 billion was bet illegally. It is further estimated that 600 million dollars of this total is bet annually with the illegal numbers game in New York.

2. In 1967, the President's Commission on Law Enforcement

and Administration of Justice estimated that illegal wagering in the United States amounted to 20 billion dollars annually, of which 6 to 7 billion dollars was believed to be profit. Since then, estimates from responsible sources have ranged as high as 60 billion dollars being wagered illegally each year.

3. There is a more recent estimate that has been made through the United States Department of Justice. According to a *New York Post* article which appeared in December 1973, the Organized Crime and Racketeering Section of the Department of Justice has been analyzing alleged stakes in illegal gambling cases investigated during a selected five-month period in 1972. Quoting from the article:

> William S. Lynch, head of the section, said prosecuted cases dealt with $1.2 billion. He estimated this at between 2 and 4 percent of the actual total, which projects to $30 to $60 billion for that short period alone. Lynch said of the $1.2 billion that it was 'a hard figure . . . I think it is the best figure ever.'

And what of *legal* wagering? Over 75 percent of the population of the United States live in jurisdictions where some form of gambling has been legalized. At the same time, a number of states, including Nebraska and Montana, are actively reviewing their previous posture concerning the legalization of various forms of gambling.

Lotteries are presently in vogue, a phenomenon started by New Hampshire's pioneering effort in 1964 and now spreading westward. Today there are eight states with government-operated legal lotteries. At least six other states are actively studying, or are in the process of implementing, such lotteries. It is interesting to note that proceeds from the recently authorized lottery in Illinois may be earmarked to help fund a public authority which will be responsible for coordinating and financing mass transportation in the Chicago urban area.[3] While a number of states have in recent years removed constitutional prohibitions against lotteries, in Colorado two proposals aimed at permitting lotteries were turned down by the people in 1972. In September 1973 a Louisiana study recommended against implementation of a lottery at the present time. In South Dakota, a privately operated, statewide lottery began in the fall of 1972, but had to cease operations after action by the State Attorney General's office.

At least three other jurisdictions—New Jersey, New York, and the District of Columbia—are exploring the legalization of the numbers game. It was announced in December 1973 that both New Jersey and New York are seriously considering the institution of a legal numbers game as a more effective means of competing with the illegal game and as an attempt to bolster sagging sales in existing legal lotteries.

The "Futures Group" is a private research organization which has been conducting a study of the socio-economic consequences of legalized gambling, pursuant to a grant from the National Science Foundation. Its preliminary findings suggest that while eight states now have lotteries which cover some 29 percent of the country's population, by 1976 there may well be lotteries in some eighteen states, covering more than 55 percent of the country's population.

In the same way that acceptability of the lottery has no doubt been enhanced by the availability of mechanized controls, especially through use of computerization, legalization of horseracing was greatly aided by the development of the pari-mutuel system, where bettors wager against each other instead of against the bookmaker. In 1928, an electronic totalizator became capable of calculating the changing odds on each horse according to the amounts bet on each, compared to the total pool. In the 1930s, automatic pari-mutuel betting spread throughout American racetracks.

Pari-mutuel betting on horseracing is the most visible form of legalized gambling. It is currently permitted, on track, in some thirty states. In addition, Virginia and Oklahoma are investigating legalization. Pari-mutuel betting on dogracing currently exists in nine states, Alabama and New Hampshire having joined the ranks in 1973; at least four other states are actively considering the introduction of this sport and its related gambling. Florida and Nevada are the two states which currently permit pari-mutuel betting on jai alai, while Connecticut and Rhode Island appear to be rapidly moving in this direction. In the latter case, the intention is not only to generate revenues through the taxation of the legalized gambling, but also to increase tourism at the famous resort city of Newport, Rhode Island.

Off-track betting, much in vogue in many other countries around the world, is now under active experimentation in the United States. Previously the private domain of the legal book-makers in Nevada and the illegal bookmakers everywhere else, off-track pari-mutuel betting on horseracing is now permissible in New York State under a regional form of local option, and has been authorized in Connecticut with the start of betting slated for 1974 to 1975. While the Connecticut Legislature also authorized the introduction of horseracing into that state, the present impetus has been to build a number of elaborate theaters, to be known as "mini-tracks," equipped with giant screens upon which would be shown live races from racetracks in other states. In addition to New York and Connecticut, at least seven states are actively exploring pari-mutuel off-track betting, although affirmative legislation before 1976 is unlikely.

Concerning sports betting, no state seems close to experimentation with the kind referred to as "head-to-head" sports betting, the kind most familiar in the United States. However, Massachusetts is considering the legalization of sports pool cards, previously defeated in the 1973 legislative session.

Of course, Nevada permits privately run head-to-head sports betting, as well as privately run casino gambling. Maryland had permitted legalized slot machines in certain counties, but does so no longer. Both New York and New Jersey have considered the institution of casino gambling, as an aid to certain economically depressed resort areas of these states. Various forms of bingo or carnival games are allowed in many states. California has card rooms by local option. Hawaii legalized social gambling in 1972. The state of Wyoming has recently approved pari-mutuel betting for professional roping events.

Legalization Options

It is clear, then, that a number of states have gambled on legalized gambling. Why? What are the interests which can legitimately be served through the legalization of one or more forms of gambling? Or what problems can be solved through legalization?

Let us first look at the effect that a properly structured legal gambling enterprise might have on organized crime, illegal gambling, and the correlative evils which flow from it. Howard Samuels, first Chairman of the Board of the New York City Off-Track Betting Corporation as well as that Corporation's first President, was recently quoted in the *New York Post:*

> You have to accept the premise that legalization has some negatives. . . . Some people who can't afford it will get involved and some will become addicted, so you have to look at it like Prohibition: [Prohibition was] an attempt to dictate morality, and that opens it up for organized crime. Who is to dictate what is moral or immoral? When Society tries to, with an unenforceable law, it aids organized crime.

Thus, legalization would automatically end the monopolistic franchise otherwise held by the illegal game. And this is important. In November 1972, the Fund for the City of New York released a report it had sponsored entitled "Legal Gambling in New York: A Discussion of Numbers and Sports Betting."

One major aspect of this study was a survey conducted by the Oliver Quayle firm. Among other things, the Quayle Survey indicated that 85 percent of bettors who bet on sporting events through bookmakers, *would* be in favor of the legalization of sports betting. This is so despite the fact that most bettors believe (incorrectly) that legalized betting would not give better odds than are now received from bookies. In other words, people would consider switching from their bookmaker to a legal gambling enterprise even if the legal game were not better than what is offered by the bookmaker. So it would seem at least theoretically feasible to favorably compete with an illegal game, and it may well be worth the effort, because any lowering of the illegal gross profits or raising of the illegal costs, makes it that much harder to finance illegal enterprises such as narcotics or loan-sharking, or to fund the invasion of legitimate businesses.

Legalization of gambling is not necessarily a panacea for the realization of this or any other goal. But there are legitimate ends to be served through legalization, with some reasonable chance of achieving some success. New York's off-track betting experiment is limited to horse betting, whereas some 85 percent of the bookmaking business in New York City appears to be on sports other than horseracing. There is some good evidence that in the limited area of competition which falls within the present OTB mandate, the presence of the legal game is being felt.

The next legitimate "goal" to be mentioned would be the raising of revenue for the support of government-approved functions. (One of the results of governmental involvement in legalized gambling could conceivably be a reduction, rather than an increase, in state revenues. This could happen, for instance, if the government decided to be a bookmaker, and chose an incompetent to determine the official point spread).

One of New York's reasons for adopting OTB (and the lottery, for that matter) was as an attempt to generate supplemental, incremental revenue not otherwise easily achievable or politically palatable through other means. There is no question but that, while as a percentage of the total state budget the amount of revenue so generated is small, in terms of absolute dollars the figure is very healthy indeed. For example, in the fiscal year ending June 30, 1973, OTB business consisted of a total handle of just under 600 million dollars, of which 14 million dollars went to the racing industry and 42 million dollars was available to local and state governments. In the current fiscal year ending June 30, 1974, we have projected a total handle of in excess of three-quarters of a billion dollars, which is expected to result in some 30 million dollars available for the racing industry and 57 million dollars for government revenue. The city of Schenectady, New York, with a population of 78,000 and a betting population base of 200,000 took its first OTB bet on July 24, 1972, paid back its start-up costs of $142,000 by the end of 1972, and achieved a profit of $559,000 for the first eleven months. The share of Schenectady OTB profits which is earmarked for the locality (amounting to approximately three percent of the city's budget) has permitted that city to lower the proposed increase in its property tax base from $3.60 per one thousand dollars of assessed valuation to 60¢ per thousand dollars. In addition, an existing refuse collection tax was able to be repealed.

Another reason for considering legalization is perhaps the most compelling: as strongly suggested by the huge volume of illegal betting in the country, the public wants to bet and will find the means of achieving this form of self-entertainment even if the public purse receives nothing from it. There are few jurisdictions in this country today with a true moral fervor against gambling.

In any event there is, fortunately, an easy answer both to those who call upon the citizenry to oppose legalization on moral grounds, or the legislator who is afraid that if he votes for legalization he is so far ahead of his constituents' desires that he is committing political suicide. That solution is to include within the enabling legislation the requirement of a referendum—perhaps both state-wide and if this passed, on a local option basis (in New York for off-track betting, no local referendum was necessary unless there were a successful petitioning effort by local forces opposed to the legalization)—the referendum to be held before legalization were allowed to come about. This would give everyone his say, and get the legislator off the hook. For if it should turn out that the public does like to gamble as a form of entertainment, and would like to be able to do it legally, then certainly no legislator could long be criticized for helping his constituents get exactly what they want.

In New York City in 1963, in an exploratory referendum, the people voted 3 to 1 in favor of off-track betting. (Enabling legislation was not passed until 1970.) In New Hampshire, the enabling legislation for the new state lottery called for the question of legalization to be automatically reviewed by means of periodic referenda. The initial approval was voted by the people, by a vote of three to one. Two years later, after initial experience with the lottery sweepstakes, the vote was five to one. Again two years later there was yet another referendum, and the vote in this one was seven to one. At this point it was deemed unnecessary to hold further referenda unless specifically requested in the future.

In other words, through the use of such referenda, the people themselves can decide whether it is all right to bet at the racetrack but not at the street corner, or whether bingo at the churches is acceptable but lottery at the candy store is not.

People are constantly gambling, whether it is card playing, bingo, the stock market, or on football games. Since this is so, it might even be an act of morality

. . . for government to recognize the way people feel about gambling today, and to legalize certain forms to be operated by governmental institutions, rather than to force people to gamble in the unregulated and ruthless domain of organized crime.

We must also consider the effect of legalization on other aspects of the economy. The lack of legalization has the effect of channeling the gambling dollar to two sources: to illegal operators and to jurisdictions where gambling is legal, particularly the state of Nevada and numerous foreign countries. In the East, there is economic pressure on those states without a lottery, to provide one, so as not to lose out to their neighboring states which do have one. The loss of capital or revenues within a particular state, to either legal or illegal sources, can certainly not be a good thing economically for the state which is losing this capital.

Thus, both legalization and the lack of it have measurable effects on the economy of the jurisdiction in question. It should be recalled that since gambling was not prohibited at common law, "laissez-faire" economics would not require the prohibition of gambling institutions, but would permit them. Thus, it cannot be viewed as an act of necessary government policy to leave prohibitory legislation on the statute rolls and let the economic consequences proceed wherever they may.

When off-track betting was legalized in New York State, there was a nearly universal outcry by the existing facets of the racing industry that racing in the Empire State was ruined and would soon be either third-rate or out of business altogether. The results, to date, demonstrate that OTB and the other parts of the industry, working in close concert, can in many ways be a distinct asset to racing, although admittedly there are some ways in which traditional on-track patterns have been affected. The economic consequences have included one or two years of economic difficulty for the traditional racing interests (although whether due to the advent of OTB or to other factors such as general economic conditions, grumblings about scandals in horseracing, etc., is a hotly debated topic); however, with off-track betting now a mature entity in New York City, purses have reached record proportions, thanks to the supplemental dollars which have flowed from the off-track handle, and the track owners are either holding their own or doing better than before. Indeed, in the wake of the "energy crisis," with many of the New York tracks virtually accessible only by car, an opinion has been voiced—not by OTB representatives—that the existence of betting parlors within the urban center may well prove to have been a decisive factor in the racing industry's effort to weather this new crisis.

It is true that, because of many factors including OTB, the tracks have felt it unnecessary to retain as many employees on-track as previously and a loss of some jobs has resulted. However, two comments need to be made here: first, OTB recognized early that it might have some responsibility in this area and entered into "Job Security Agreements" with the on-track unions, which provide some measure of protection to the on-track employees. Second, at the same time that the racetracks in the New York area have laid off perhaps several hundred employees over the last three years—for all sorts of reasons, during that same period the new industry of off-track betting has been created which directly employs almost three thousand workers: as of December 31, 1973, OTB employed 2,711 persons, of which 1,803 were full-time and 908 were part-time. In addition, OTB has paid out millions upon millions of dollars as "expenses"—payment to vendors and contractors for building our branches, providing betting tickets, and all the other aspects of a large corporation's accounts payable, that you might expect. It should also be noted that in the case of state lotteries, lottery agents, who will usually be local store owners, receive a commission for selling the tickets.

So the concept of a legal gambling institution as a "positive economic multiplier" is certainly not one to take lightly. One further note: in addition to OTB's payments to New York tracks, last year we gave half a million dollars to the state of Maryland, for that state's cooperation in the effort by New York City OTB to take bets on Maryland races during the winter months. It is estimated that this year's share to the State of Maryland will exceed one million dollars.

All of the economic consequences of legalization are not necessarily positive. First of all, it is necessary to conduct some sort of return-on-investment analysis, to determine the economic viability of the initial investment. For instance, would casino gambling thrive in the face of the long-established competition from a neighbor state? Such a factor must be a major consideration in determining which forms of gambling should be legalized.

Further analysis would have to be considered on the likely effects of legalization on personal and private capital. On the positive side are the possible increases in available personal income: through prize money, new salaries, or less taxes (or more realistically, less increases in taxes). On the negative side will be the nonwinners, or the potential loss of jobs in affected "alternative" or "competitive" product industries, including the loss of employment to employees of the illegal game (a not-to-be-taken-lightly sociological question, in the case, for instance, of the numbers runners in the ghetto areas of New York and other similar cities, where such employment may well be an integral component in the present make-up of the sociological framework of such communities.) A further negative would be present if the bettor were to lose more than he could afford as part of his entertainment dollar. On the other hand, some shopkeepers in New York City have stated that they love having an Off-Track Betting parlor as a neighbor, since it increases the flow of people to their block and ends up increasing sales. Again, we see an issue neither black nor white.

From the evidence and studies to date, based upon both OTB and the lotteries, there does not appear to be any reason to believe that the vast majority of wagering done on these legal forms of betting is other than moderate. In fact, what does appear to be happening is that to some extent a percentage of the entertainment dollar is being redirected.

One of the problems previously touched upon needs emphasis: in a jurisdiction where one or more forms of gambling are already legal (for instance, horseracing) the concept of legalizing another form (for instance, off-track betting or the lottery) must be viewed in terms of its economic effect on the already existing, indigenous enterprise. While the franchise to operate a racetrack has been held by the courts of a number of states to be a privilege and not a right, and thus one about which the legislature has a right to change the ground rules or to eliminate altogether, such action must not be taken lightly and if done, must be done with eyes open. (However, off-track betting could even be structured so as to aid racing as its primary purpose.) In New York, when OTB was legalized, it is questionable whether the existing industry was sufficiently considered, and so the legislation has had to be amended a number of times. In this context, there is an interesting example: when dog racing was legalized in one of the states of Australia where horseracing was well established, a certain percentage of the take from dog racing was earmarked for the benefit of horseracing, so as not to unduly damage that major and existing industry.

I have suggested a number of "goals" of legalization: competition with illegal gambling; production of revenues for the support of governmental functions; the desire of the populace for this form of entertainment; the economic multiplier; and the effect on the indigenous industry. It is very likely close to impossible to structure a situation where all these goals can be achieved; some might have to be sacrificed, or some negatives might have to be permitted in order to enhance the likelihood of achieving others of these "goals."

Rufus King, a Washington attorney and a noted expert in the area of gambling and organized crime, recently put it this way:

. . . You can't have it both ways. If you are going to legalize gambling to raise revenue, then you are not going to make much of a dent in organized crime [and its] illegal gambling activities. . . . In numbers operations . . . you have to give a good deal more where there is already illegal gambling play, so if the purpose is to go after crime, then pretty much forget revenue. On the other hand, if it's to go after revenue, then pretty much don't count on your operations to affect crime.[4]

It is certainly true that the strongest competition with an illegal game would be to return more winnings to the bettors than the illegal game does, but this obviously would be at the expense of the maximum production of revenue for government. It is this same kind of analysis which the legislature or racing commission must go through, when it determines what portion of the retained share of the betting dollar will be kept by the racing industry for expenses, expansion and profit, and what portion will be available as revenue for government.

Of course, this again is not black or white. But it is an important factor, and one which must not only affect a decision whether to legalize, but what to legalize.

Different Gambling Games

It would be useful to comment briefly on the various sorts of games which are available, and some of their differences.[5] Is your primary goal to compete with illegal gambling? Then you might introduce only those games which presently raise such a problem, and which have the best chance of successfully competing, such as a daily, pick-your-own-numbers game rather than a different type of lottery format.

Is your goal to give the bettors the entertainment opportunities they wish consistent with your social policy? Then look for games with active bettor participation, such as racing, cards or sports betting, where a bettor can affect his chances of winning through skill or knowledge. In addition, there are those forms of gambling described as "pseudo-active" as opposed to "passive," where a bettor has a sense of participation even if skill is not involved. In this latter category would be placed casino games, slot machines, and the numbers game as differentiated from the other forms of lotteries or raffles. Look, also, to those games with a high return to the bettor in terms of the prize structure.

If you are interested in maintaining the most stringent administrative and security controls, then you will probably stay away from casinos or legalized bookmaking. Even bingo can present administrative headaches in the accurate receipt of revenue and expense information. On the other hand, computer-controlled government-operated lotteries, sports pools, or pari-mutuel wagering all contain fine control mechanisms.

Do you wish to minimize operator risk? Then do not give

credit, do not get involved with high-investment low-net games before you totally understand the degree of customer acceptance and the actual scope of your available market, and do not start a game involving "pick-your-own" by the bettor in a non-pari-mutuel environment; in other words, do not get involved in head-to-head sports betting as a bookmaker does it, or in the numbers game in a low-volume environment with no limit on the total percentage of the pool which can end up on a single number. In contrast, the low-risk games include pari-mutuel operations and most of the present experimentation with lotteries.

Let me list the types of elements just discussed: degree of bettor participation; prize structure; do additional bets increase the size of your prize, or just increase your chances of winning the same prize; amount of prize pay-back per betting dollar; the chances of being some kind of a winner; amount of operator or governmental "profit" per betting dollar; amount of risk to the operator; length of interval between betting events; investment; social problems; law enforcement problems; administrative and security control problems; familiarity by the potential bettor with the proposed game; other opportunities to play the proposed game; and finally, start-up time to get into business.

The New York Example

My own business, The New York City Off-Track Betting Corporation, deserves some comment as an example. We were created by the New York State Legislature as a Public Benefit Corporation; that is, we have a corporate structure with a Board of Directors and a president. Our net revenues after expenses are available for distribution, sort of as "dividends," to the state of New York and the city of New York, for governmental purposes. We do, however, have many restrictions, such as public purchasing procedures and Civil Service. In short, we are a governmental organization run as much as possible like a private enterprise, but not a privately owned business. The public nature of the enterprise is such that we must always be prepared to make some compromises with the traditional view of the profit motive.

Bets are placed with OTB either through Telephone Betting Accounts which are similar in operation to checking accounts (no credit), or cash-and-carry at our betting windows at some 120 offices throughout the city of New York. Unlike at most tracks, our on-line real-time computer system permits any window to both sell tickets and cash winning bets, as well as take bets on all races, at more than one track, for simple or exotic types of wagers, all at the same time. The computer system has also provided us with the capability of generating a unique serial number on each individual ticket, virtually eliminating the danger of mass counterfeiting, and greatly reducing the possibility of successful ticket alteration. Each day we are doing business on two or more tracks, everything from win betting to triple (or trifecta) betting, and we have been averaging a daily handle of in excess of 2.5 million dollars, with over 4 million dollars in cash changing hands back and forth each day.

When a customer wants to make a bet, the information about the bet is keyed into one of our betting terminals, and the data is transmitted to our Central Computer Facility by high speed data lines. The Central Computer processes the bet and transmits necessary information back to the branch office terminal, where a ticket is printed.

All bets in each betting pool are combined by the Central Processing Facility and processed through OTBC Computer Communications Systems to the various in-state tracks. The Corporation maintains its own computer facility at each in-state track to receive these transmissions from Central, so that the betting information can be combined with the on-track Pari-Mutuel Systems, resulting in one uniform payout price which is paid both on and off track.

The Central Processing System operates identically for out-of-state betting pools except that present federal law apparently prohibits transmission of bets across state lines; therefore, the Corporation maintains its own pools and calculates its own prices for out-of-state racing.

Various vendors of off-track betting systems are now prepared to provide already developed OTB systems for relatively easy conversion to the needs of new jurisdictions. These vendors will accept payment for such a system, including necessary computers, computer operators, and betting terminals, by means of a percent of gross handle or transaction charge of so many cents per transaction, in lieu of standard purchasing or leasing arrangements. Thus, the investment needed or risk involved in going into off-track betting has been greatly alleviated, and the start-up time cut to one year, or less depending on how far planning has advanced at the time of a commitment to proceed.

In sum, the criminal justice system deserves to do itself the favor of considering carefully a partial or total legalization of gambling along the lines and options presented here. By so doing, we may well put our enforcement resources to better use.

NOTES

1. Chicago Crime Commission and ITT Research Institute. *A Study of Organized Crime in Illinois—Summary:* 1971. p. 27.
2. The primary source for this lottery history is John Samuel Ezell, *Fortune's Merry Wheel* (Cambridge, Mass.: Harvard University Press, 1960).
3. This earmarking did not occur.
4. *Proceedings of the National Conference on Public Gaming.* (July 10-12, 1973) NLW Advisory, Inc. (Boca Raton, Fla.: 1973). p. 23.
5. The primary source for this section is material prepared by Mathematica, Inc. (Princeton, N.J.) for The Futures Group study *The Impact of Legalized Gambling,* New York: Praeger, 1974).

RUDOLPH J. GERBER

3. OBSCENITY
—LUST'S LABORS LOST AND WON

"So first she tasted the porridge of the Great, Huge Bear, and that was too hot for her; and she said a bad word about that."
—from the original version of "The Three Bears" by Robert Southey.

Even Goldilocks, the heroine of Robert Southey's "The Three Bears," said obscenities. Ever since the story came off the press in 1834 those obscenities have been deleted, so that the words she uttered remain a literary secret. Like Goldilocks, former President Nixon utters official obscenities and, like Southey's censors, he hides them from the public. Unlike Goldilocks, however, the Nixon-Ford Administration has proposed to Congress a new Federal Criminal Code making any explicit representation of the sex act, written or pictorial, criminally obscene. To complicate the landscape, the Supreme Court has refueled the debate with a new geographical approach to obscenity. Pornography, long enshrined in the groin of the beholder, has now become a pain in the neck for the criminal justice system.

Opposing camps have long girded themselves for this tireless battle. On one side are the Decent People (police, churchgoers, parents) who see the flood of pornography contributing to a new fall of Rome. To them, all pornography from profanity to nudity to sex shops must be rooted out to preserve the pristine lacework of the neuter mind. This group solemnly intones the chant that nations are born stoic and die epicurean. In the other camp are the Libertarians (law professors, ACLU, and hairy bohemians) who see their novel art forms endangered by repres-

Rudolph J. Gerber is Associate Director of the Criminal Code Commission of Arizona and teaches Criminal Law and Criminal Justice at Arizona State University.

sive legislation. Allen Ginsberg, poet laureate of pornographers, expresses a liberal version of this Libertarian creed: "Who cares if people want to copulate in public on TV? Why Not? The controllers can always turn off the screen." The two camps debate like ships passing in the night, without knowing what they are fighting over—a problem acutely shared by law enforcement agencies and courts.

Both the Administration's and the Supreme Court's current proposals on obscenity, different as they are, raise the central issue whether obscenity constitutes a greater threat to the community than the censorship machinery it manufactures. An easier judgment is that the Supreme Court's 1973–74 obscenity decisions are impractical. Former Attorney General Ramsey Clark views them as "hypocritical, inhumane, unenforceable, and unconstitutional." A Winchester, Indiana obscenity statute, modeled on the 1973 obscenity decisions, could not be printed in the local county newspaper because its anatomical definitions were too obscene for the community press. To implement the local community standards endorsed by the court, the town of Clarkstown, New York, recently appointed a blind man as movie censor. Community standards in differing locales have both approved and proscribed *Playboy* Magazine, the films *The Devil in Miss Jones*, and *Deep Throat*, as well as bringing under attack Heller's *Catch-22*, Salinger's *Catcher in the Rye*, Dickey's *Deliverance*, Steinbeck's *Grapes of Wrath*, Brown's *Manchild in the Promised Land*, and Morris's *Naked Ape*. Yet the 1973–74 Court decisions offer seeds of compromise between censorship and free expression, but at the price of junking the present approach to obscenity for a more economical and realistic tactic.

The 1973-74 Obscenity Decisions: "One Nation, Divisible . . . with Pornography for Some."

The Supreme Court's obscenity opinions in 1973–74 produced tightened restraints on obscenity. The restrictive decisions were a surprise; there had been suggestions of differing standards for juveniles and adults. Instead, a new course was set by the 1973–74 decisions, a route which promises to raise as many obstacles as it surmounts. In Miller v. California, Chief Justice Burger defined the new test as follows:

The basic guidelines for the trier of fact must be, (a) whether the average person, applying contemporary community standards would find that the work, taken as a whole, appeals to the prurient interest, (b) whether the work depicts or describes, in a patently offensive way, sexual conduct specifically defined by the applicable state law, and (c) whether the work, taken as a whole, lacks serious literary, artistic, political, or scientific value.[1]

To appreciate the new Miller test, it is helpful briefly to summarize its 1973 companion cases, which, unlike Miller, focused not on definition but circumstance. In Paris Adult Theatre I v. Slaton,[2] the Court upheld state power to prohibit showing obscene films in places of public accommodation, regardless of whether the showing is limited to consenting adults. In United States v. 12,200-Ft.[3] Reels of Super 8MM. Film, the Court upheld federal power to prohibit the importation of obscene material for private, personal use and possession only. United States v. Orito[4] upheld governmental power to prohibit the transportation of obscene material in interstate commerce, regardless of whether the material was only intended for the private use of the transporter or whether its transport was by private carriage. In Kaplan v. California[5] the Court upheld the power of government to regulate nonpictorial obscenity (a book, *Suite 69*, with no pictorial content) just as it regulates pictorial obscenity.

Excerpts from the Kaplan and Paris decisions are of mixed blood. In Paris, the Court states that the legislature may assume obscenity leads to antisocial acts, although that has not yet been so proven (implicitly assuming that it will be so proven). In Kaplan, the Court, in effect, states that such proof is unnecessary since the causal assumption is not subject to test. Facetious minds might suggest that the Court did not wish to be confused with the real facts. The more gentlemanly analysis, of course, is that the Court meant only to insure the states' powers to legislate in the absence of conclusive empirical data.

Serious problems arise with the Court's new interplay between social value and community standards. The older requirement that material be "utterly without redeeming social value" now yields to a stricter requirement that the work, taken as a whole, lack "serious" literary, artistic, political, or scientific value. What is meant by "serious" value is unclear. The Court observed that the old test placed on the prosecution a negative burden virtually impossible to discharge. Replacing one negative with a newer one hardly makes the burden of proving any negative any easier. Now, in any case, only "serious" values are protected, and these serious values must permeate the work as a whole. Incidental serious value is not salvific.

There are also feudalistic connotations surrounding the community standards issue. It is no easier, of course, to determine the common denominator for obscenity within any one state than among the many states. Since "seriousness" is now measured by the local community standards of the "average" person in his own hamlet, the new obscenity cases imply that some academic works may well be found obscene merely because some average persons in the local community find the esoteric value of obscenity not sufficiently serious to warrant protection. Puritan localities may now impose restrictive verdicts on the average nonpuritans in other parts of the state. Ambitious prosecutors may begin their obscenity cases in small, puritan fiefs and then urge that their victories are res judicata for the entire state. It was precisely this parochial standard that Georgia officials exploited successfully to prosecute the movie *Carnal Knowledge,* illustrating how the local standards within the state of Georgia vary drastically from one fiefdom to another.

In this sense, federalism falls victim to feudalism in the new decisions. In certain important constitutional respects, moral power of the courts has flowed recently to the center, away from the states. In interstate commerce and civil rights, Congress and Court in the recent past have sought to assure one nation free of balkanizing state influences in favor of nationwide uniformity, under the conviction that school segregation, search and seizure, privacy and free expression should not be left to the unchecked eccentricities of local legislatures. Under the new obscenity cases, however, the fifty states may now fix their own peculiar criteria to impede entry of ideas expressed in books, magazines, films, and plays; indeed, the nation's 78,200 local hamlets now may erect their own toll gates.

To give final authority to local censors increases rather than avoids the problems of giving fair, consistent notice to publishers of what they cannot print and transport. Notice becomes grist in Miller's mill. According to *Playboy* publisher Hugh Hefner:

What we are faced with—all magazine publishers, book publishers, national newspapers, film producers—is that curious problem of how to produce materials for a national audience when censorship is turned back into a local option situation.

The two major 1974 censorship decisions by the Court confirm the status of this country as a censors' checkerboard. Jenkins v. Georgia[6] holds, contrary to the Georgia Supreme Court, that the film *Carnal Knowledge* is not obscene. While that film gets a free pass, it is valid for that film alone. In an uncomfortable review of Miller, the Court states that local juries do not have "unbridled" discretion in determining what is obscene. Jenkins insists that local juries continue to root their obscenity judgments in their own local standards, which, of course, is precisely what the original *Carnal Knowledge* jury had accurately done in Albany, Georgia. The Jenkins Justices merely disagreed with those standards. In repudiating those standards, however, the Court gave no help for aligning to its standard the artistic eccentricities of other locales judging other materials. Jenkins's 1974 companion, Hambling v. United States, blandly reaffirms the competency of local juries:

A juror is entitled to draw on his own knowledge of the views of the average person in the community or vicinage from which he comes for making the required determination, just as he is entitled to draw on his own knowledge of the propensities of a 'reasonable' person in other areas of the law.[7]

Read in conjunction with Jenkins, Hambling thus bestows approval on the Jury's articulation of the "average," "reasonable" responses of its "community." But obscenity, the Court notwithstanding, remains a most unaverageable commodity about which reasonable men have differed to the point of extremes of non-community. While approving of local jury standards, Jenkins and Hambling proceed to warn that these local judgments must be "bridled." But why a bridle if the jury of good and true men are accurate reflections of the "average" and "reasonable" views of its hamlet? The Supreme Court articulates no bridle; indeed, it reserves the undescribed bridle magiclike for its own use. Clearly, then, the local jury is "bridled" into more enlightened standards only via the Super Censors' imposition of an unarticulated quasi-national standard in place of the standards of the good and true men of the "vicinage." The Court has thus applauded with the left hand [Hambling] that same local discretion which it has faulted with its right hand [Jenkins]. In the future, the well-founded but restrictive judgments of local juries will be "bridled" by the Supreme Board of Censors, whose 1973–74 decisions reserve to it the albatross of case-by-case "nationalizing" of the local eccentricities it has endorsed in Miller, Jenkins, and Hambling. The 1973–74 decisions become, alas, as decipherable as a doctor's prescription, less likely to induce a cure than a relapse for the country's intractable obscenity malaise.

Research on Causality

The first step toward sanity in obscenity is realizing with the eleven-volume 1970 Report of the Commission on Pornography and Obscenity that there is no discernible connection between pornography and sex crime—indeed, with crime of any sort. Recent research yields the same effect. The most significant study since 1970 on the alleged social harm of pornography comes from Goldstein and Kant, *Pornography and Sexual Deviance,* published in 1973. The work developed as an extension of the authors' research project for the Pornography Commission.

One of their first major discoveries is the tendency by sex offenders to generate their own pornography ex nihilo. Sex offenders, and those prone to such activity, typically read sexual meanings into material devoid of such meanings for the normal person.

A second finding buttresses older conclusions: sex offenders report consistently less frequent exposure to erotica and more sex guilt. Rather than being surfeited with pornography, the typical sex offender comes from a sexually repressed environment permitting less than average exposure to and expression of sexuality. A third discovery is that erotica serves different goals for adults and juveniles. For the latter, pornography is educational as well as exciting. For adults, however, it maintains sexual interest and arousal but rarely alters established behavior patterns.

As sex offenders themselves, the authors found little, if any, evidence to suggest that exposure to erotica tends to ignite antisocial sexual behavior. Rather, the pronounced sexual guilt of the sex offender seems to inhibit overt imitation of the behavior beyond a commonplace tendency to masturbate. The normally developing male, by contrast, readily substitutes real women for masturbation and fantasy. In the words of the authors:

. . . [T]here is some evidence that for rapists, exposure to erotica portraying 'normal' heterosexual relations can serve to ward off antisocial sexual impulses. . . . [g]reater and earlier exposure to erotic material might have been educational and lessened the development of antisocial and deviant attitudes and behavior in persons so disposed.

In essence, this most recent research supports the 1970 conclusions of the Presidential Pornography Commission and places the question on a political-legal level: will the public and its courts permit a more sensible approach to pornography than the incredible waste involved in the present absolutist scheme?

Wasted Time and Money

Obscenity trials are one of the major consequences of using criminal sanctions to eliminate distribution of explicit material to adults.[8] Criminal sanctions in an area so open to debate raise a constitutional issue in almost every case. Furthermore, because of the public's extensive patronage of the adult materials industry, defendants in obscenity cases rarely have difficulty paying the expensive legal fees for raising these constitutional issues. So long as distribution of obscenity to forewarned adults is criminalized, protracted and inconclusive litigation continues to occupy the courts.

Not only courts are caught in the obscenity quagmire. Law enforcement agencies and prosecution offices suffer intractable problems because of the current obscenity law. The experience of the Los Angeles City Attorney's Office illustrates the typical difficulties in using criminal sanctions to eliminate the adult materials industry.

To understand the problems in the current obscenity laws, it helps to know something of the structure of the adult materials industry. Most establishments which distribute adult materials do so through a system of absentee ownership. An adult bookstore in Hollywood may well be owned by a California corporation whose owners and officers are Texas residents who never set foot in California.

Absentee ownership is a crucial factor in the frustration of obscenity law enforcement. Only those persons who have knowledge of the contents, nature, and character of the matter sold or displayed on their premises can be criminally charged with its distribution. Such knowledge is exceedingly difficult, if not impossible, to establish for absentee owners. Cases filed thus tend to prosecute employees of absentee owners, not the owners themselves. If an employee is convicted, he seeks other employment. Another employee is then quickly hired. The distribution of the material continues despite innumerable convictions of employees because the industry can easily bear the musical-chair of conviction and replacement of local employees.

Even in those rare instances where a case can be made against an owner, inordinate amounts of police investigatory time are required. The police must identify the true owner and establish that he does have the requisite knowledge. Often they must track the owner down and read him a statement as to the nature of the business his establishment carries on, so as to impute knowledge to him.

The practical result of this is that obscenity prosecutions are more shadow than substance. Despite extensive prosecution efforts by the Los Angeles City Attorney's office, the adult materials industry still thrives in Los Angeles, which now is possibly the pornography capital of the country. Innumerable and endless convictions of clerks, ticket sellers, and popcorn vendors have not markedly diminished the distribution of adult materials but have wasted law enforcement and prosecution resources that could better deter serious crimes against persons and property.

Adding to the practical difficulties of obscenity law enforcement is the fact that public attitudes towards adult materials are changing. As a result, jurors are becoming more reluctant to convict in cases that involve distribution of materials to adults who know what they are seeing or buying. Jurors are reluctant to convict when they have themselves patronized the materials at issue.

Mixed results in obscenity prosecutions have occurred all over the country. Results in *Deep Throat* prosecutions are particularly interesting, as that film depicts graphic sexual activity for approximately fifty minutes of its sixty-two-minute running time. In California, no jury has convicted a defendant under Section 311 for distributing or exhibiting *Deep Throat*. Numerous attempts have been made. The Los Angeles County District Attorney's Office recently dismissed charges against the film after a trial consuming several months, and an estimated quarter of a million dollars, resulted in only a hung jury. Prosecutions against distributors or exhibitors of *Deep Throat* have resulted in jury verdicts of acquittal in Downey and Ontario. Outside California, prosecutions against *Deep Throat* have yielded acquittals or hung juries in communities across the country as diverse as Binghampton, New York; Cincinnati, Ohio; Houston, Texas; and Sioux Falls, South Dakota. Prosecutors nationwide have had similar difficulty in obtaining convictions in cases involving *Behind the Green Door* and *The Devil in Miss Jones*.

In light of the negligible effect of obscenity prosecutions and the growing public tolerance of the right of forewarned adults to see what they want, the question now really is whether the resources directed to obscenity prosecutions could be better utilized in the fight against the ever-increasing menace of crimes against persons and property.

The manpower costs of prosecution are considerable. A police officer must spend at least one full day on the most simple obscenity case involving a search warrant. Far more investigatory time is required in prosecution of absentee owners of adult materials stores or movie houses. In addition, from one-half to two days court time is required for the investigating officer's testimony if a case goes to trial. Prosecutorial time includes at least a one-half working day in an attempt to negotiate a plea bargain and a staggering two to five weeks to try a contested case. The judicial time involved is substantially identical. The inevitable appeal from a conviction requires at least three days of attorney time to prepare. Overall, according to the Los Angeles City Attorney's Office, the total governmental costs for typical contested obscenity prosecutions lie somewhere between 10 and 25 thousand dollars per case.

Given the expense, frustration, and uncertainty involved in obscenity prosecutions, it is not surprising that many prosecution offices are reexamining their value in light of the pressing need to stem the rising level of crime against persons and property. The Sacramento County District Attorney's Office has forsworn further obscenity prosecutions and is in the process of dismissing its pending cases. The District Attorney has stated that prosecuting distributors of explicit material is "futile, frustrating and extremely costly." The San Francisco District Attorney's Office has substantially forgone obscenity prosecutions. In Pennsylvania, the Allegheny County District Attorney has made a similar decision. After two lengthy trials against *Deep Throat* ended in hung juries, Houston, Texas, prosecution officials decided not to prosecute any further obscenity cases involving quality adult entertainment films. Overall, there is a growing national trend to reexamine the value of obscenity prosecutions in light of more pressing law enforcement needs. The trend needs further stimulation if it is to survive.

One reason obscenity prosecutions are now so difficult to win is that public attitudes toward explicit adult materials have changed to the more permissive. This is demonstrated by the growing public patronage of such material. *Deep Throat,* for example, set a Los Angeles record for any type of movie exhibited at a single theater by grossing 3.2 million dollars during an eighty-one week run. Three "X-rated" films, *Deep Throat, The Devil in Miss Jones,* and *Last Tango in Paris* were among Los Angeles's top-grossing first-run movies between October 1972 and September 1973, placing first, seventh, and eighth respectively. Obviously, viewers of explicit movies and other materials are not limited to a small group of drooling perverts.

The point is that juries merely reflect a growing public tolerance of the right of adults to read and see what they want. In a recent public opinion poll conducted by the Field organization and introduced into evidence by the defense in the Los Angeles trial of *Behind the Green Door,* 52 percent of those surveyed favored the idea of allowing forewarned adults to see whatever they wanted as long as limits were placed on the advertising and promotion of explicit material. Ten percent of those surveyed favored no restrictions on the availability of explicit material to adults nor on the advertising of such material. Thus almost two-thirds of those surveyed favored unlimited availability of explicit material for adults.

Paradoxically, public patronage is in part a result of censorship. The publicity surrounding criminal prosecutions places an aura of mystery and intrigue around explicit material, thereby increasing patronage. The financial success of *Deep Throat* relates in large part to the notorious number of prosecutions brought against its exhibitors. Another cost is widespread disrespect and disregard for the law. An unenforceable, ineffective law gives the impression of erratic justice. Prohibition is a prime example of the consequences of criminalizing a product large numbers of people want. Criminal sanctions should generally be reserved for serious conduct threatening discernible harm to lives and property.

Lust's Labors Won

Somewhere in the obscenity quagmire there gleams a rough diamondlike compromise between free expression and censorship.

While no pretense is made here to have captured that elusive diamond, one of its facets suggests that legislatures qualify the outright a priori condemnation of obscenity-via-definition with more limited, variable control over a few, well-defined circumstances of commercial expression. This concept of variable obscenity, first proposed by Lockhart and McClure in 1960,[9] recommends evaluating material not per se but by its effect on differing audiences.

Two prime audiences warrant special attention: youth and the nonconsenting adult population. Protecting these two audiences while permitting, in principle, the dissemination of pornography strikes a practical balance between free expression and censorship and permits more economic law enforcement. If the censor's interests are limited to protection of juveniles and adults sensitive to inadvertent exposure to erotica, then a workable definition of obscenity would consist solely of a highly precise list of prohibited commercializations of sexual conduct. No subjective values nor emotions would be invoked; no national bridle would be clamped on local morals; indeed, no geographical standard would need to be invoked at all.

Special protection of the young is a concern as ancient as our culture. Plato and Aristotle urged that special care be taken in protecting the immature from talk and books and pictures. Most Americans believe that children should not be exposed to hardcore sexual materials. Parents want to make their own decisions regarding the suitability of such materials for their children.

If there were any doubt of the constitutional validity of prohibiting pornography to minors as a specific class, that doubt was laid to rest by the United States Supreme Court decision in Ginsberg v. New York, which holds that states have the power to regulate obscene material provided the purpose is the protection of minors:

. . . [E]ven where there is an invasion of protected freedoms the power of the state to control the conduct of children reaches beyond the scope of its authority over adults.

. . .

I think a State may permissibly determine that, at least in some precisely-delineated areas, a child—like someone in a captive audience—is not possessed of that full capacity for individual choice which is the presumption of First Amendment guarantees.[10]

Indebted in large part to similar proposals by knowledgeable draftsmen,[11] the statute below keeps the First Amendment alive and well while keeping professionals from pushing erotica on the young. It guarantees broad freedom of expression with precise restrictions on dissemination. Hopefully, it shows obscenity as a genus of expression as definable as poison ivy among other plants, but with a view not toward uprooting it but guiding it away from those areas likely to be infected by it. In effect, this statute does not ban erotica but only its availability to the young; adult access remains untouched. The statute follows:

A person commits a misdemeanor when, as either principal or agent, he sells, delivers, mails, exhibits, or displays to any minor person any material, whether pictured, animated, live, or printed, which depicts any of the following:

(1) sexual conduct, here defined as masturbation, intercourse, or other sexual contact with the sexual organs, breasts, or buttocks of any human being(s) or animal(s); or

(2) sexual excitement, here defined as the state of physical stimulation of human or animal sexual organs; or

(3) sado-masochism, here defined as flagellation or other torture by or upon a person who is nude or clad in undergarments or in any way physically restrained.

A second subarea in which limited censorship may be appropriate is that of public display. Again, there is ample legal precedent. In 1952, Justice Douglas expressed his objection to licensing radios in street cars for the reason that the people have a "right to be left alone" in public. That right would seem to entail the analogous right to walk the streets without being assailed by graphic blasts of inescapable buttocks and breasts impinging on the eyes no less inescapably than piped-in music assaults the captive ear. Air pollution, shoreline beauty, and highway aesthetics, all recognized as noble social goals, suggest kinship with an elevated moral tone on billboards, store-fronts, marquees, and store windows.

Again, there is solid legal support for such limited restraint. Rowan v. Post Office Department, banning mailing of unsolicited erotica, is highlighted by the following elaboration on privacy from Chief Justice Burger:

> The right of every person 'to be let alone' must be placed in the scales with the right of others to communicate. In today's complex society we are inescapably captive audiences for many purposes, but a sufficient measure of individual autonomy must survive to permit every householder to exercise control over unwanted mail.
>
> . . .
>
> If this prohibition operates to impede the flow of even valid ideas, the answer is that no one has a right to press even 'good' ideas on an unwilling recipient. That we are often 'captives' outside the sanctuary of the home and subject to objectionable speech and other sound does not mean we must be captives everywhere.[12]

If the Constitution and courts have created a zone of privacy in the bedroom and mailbox and street car, legislatures can readily extend that zone to protect public exposure to offensive street materials. Individuals have compelling need for areas where they can protect themselves from offensive intrusions. The public loudspeakers blaring Danish-style obscenity to captive eyes and ears of the unwilling should be silenced. Again, it is not the material as such but the circumstances of its display which need restraint. Discreet terminology and subtle labels could protect the sensitive while still harkening to the sensuous. Movie marquees might merely list "adult film" without title or posters. Adult bookstores might be only so labeled, without salacious magazine covers in their windows. Billboards and news stands should advertise their wares without the incentives of thighs, posteriors, and midriffs to assault the public's fatigued eyes. A model statute along these lines is not beyond the realm of possibility:

A person commits a misdemeanor if, acting as principal or agent, he displays or permits to be displayed in or on any store-window or along any public sidewalk or street, or depot, park or vehicle any material which depicts any of the following:

(1)   sexual conduct, here defined as masturbation, intercourse, or other sexual contact with the sexual organs, breasts, or buttocks of any human being(s) or animal(s); or

(2)   sexual excitement, here defined as the state of physical stimulation of human or animal sexual organs; or

(3)   sado-masochism, here defined as flagellation or other torture by or upon a person who is nude or clad in undergarments or in any way physically restrained; or

(4)   frontal nudity of the human male or female body, except where such a nude presentation is incidental to a recognized, bona fide medical or artistic exhibit.

It is a defense to this section that the described material was exhibited within a commercial establishment marked 'adults only,' limited to adult entry, and not visible in any way on or from the exterior of such establishment.

A second, more geographical variety of circumstantial obscenity is that of "zoned obscenity." Replacing the criminal model with a zoning model permits a zoning-out of offensive pornography from certain areas and zoning-in of such materials within limited, precisely defined areas. Boston provides a current example. There, the city fathers have designated a two-square-block area adjacent to downtown as a "Combat Zone" offering unrestricted access to erotica by adults. Other urban areas are off-limits to pornography. Juveniles are permitted access to the Combat Zone but restricted from patronizing its establishments via curfew laws and regulations on sales to minors. While there may be constitutional problems with this approach (such as the pornographer who tries to move his business to the suburbs), the zoning approach has the advantages of a more efficient, more uniform, and less penal approach to the pornography problem.

Conclusion: Paradise Regained

Three things need be said here. In the first place, courts and legislatures need to pay more credence to careful social research on the presumed harmful effects of pornography. It is not un-likely that a more sympathetic review of this data would suggest that committing rape after reading erotica is about as likely as becoming a virgin after reading about the life of Queen Elizabeth I.

Secondly, if censorship is still thought a necessity, ways to reconcile it more efficiently with the First Amendment need to be pursued in place of the outright countering of one by the other. Variable obscenity, "circumstantial" statutes, or zoning laws seem preferable to the Supreme Court's local option ap-proach which has already made the country a censor's checker-board and the criminal justice system a basket case.

Thirdly, if obscenity censorship in an absolute defining mode is still thought necessary along the lines of cases like Miller and Hambling, consistency demands that we censor the equal or greater immoralities abounding in our culture. One of the many immoral facts in this country today is that the only morality our law has been willing to censor is sexual. That is a small, perfumed corner of the trash heap on which our minds play. Conformity to sexual modesty, while important, is hardly more important than honesty, kindness, and courage. While it requires a Supreme Court decision to let Georgians view *Carnal Knowledge,* any well-heeled sponsor can let the entire nation of young and old view the graphic violence of *The Godfather* on national TV. No book has ever been suppressed because it promoted selfishness or dishonesty. Yet glorifying social injustice and napalm is at least as humanly demoralizing as the fantasized tales of cavorting sexual athletes. If censorship grows from a society's lack of confidence in its own morality, as the traditional obscenity debate suggests, that same censorship, if thought necessary, should re-strict those other immoralities beyond the sexual frontier where national self-confidence is far more eroded: the violence, racism, exploitation, and criminal profiteering presented with the leer of success to both sexes of all ages in books and the media.

Author Melvin van Peebles has said it well:

NEW OBSCENITY RULING!!!?

Lord, Lord, new rulings and here me I haven't never even run into

55

no relevant old obscenity laws.

What obscenity rules? You still can and always could show and do all the most really big obscenities on the old silver screen you wanted —from shuffling niggers rushing to massa with a mint julep, to triumphant superblacks winning with the help of law and order (massa disguised behind a badge), to Tonto getting done in (long on nobility but short on victory).

You can deal, do, show, say all and anything you please about spics, coons, wops, broads, honkeys, wasps, yids, gooks, slopes, imperialism, gangsterism, Watergate games, pacification, reallocation, megatons, methadone, and so on—what obscenity laws? We are free to deal with all the big-time perversions any way we please (with impunity, so the saying goes).

There are no obscenity laws to speak of, unless maybe you mean that pet preoccupation of some of the mainstream folks obsessed with restraining glimpses of *people doing it* and associable genitalia. The topsy-turvines of their priorities is a clue to where their heads are. The absurdity of a mentality that puts pubic hair over laissez-faire, sex over self-hate-fostering stereotypes—that's insanity!

When Third World folks and disenfranchised youth are struggling for perspective on their existence, to have some folks pushing their pet coital obsession and coming on righteous behind it, to boot— that's obscenity. New rulings, Old rulings, Whose rulings—not mine.

Fred Douglass laid it out a long time ago when he said the master ain't got no laws, national or local, a slave oughta feel duty bound to respect.[13]

NOTES

1. 413 U.S. 24 (1973)
2. 413 U.S. 49 (1973)
3. 413 U.S. 123 (1973)
4. 413 U.S. 139 (1973)
5. 413 U.S. 115 (1973)
6. 41 L. Ed. 2d. 642 (1974)
7. 41 L. Ed. 2d. 590, 613 (1974)
8. Much of this material is indebted to research by the Los Angeles City Prosecutor's Office.
9. Lockhard and McClure, *Censorship of Obscenity,* 45 Minn. L.R. 5, 77 (1960), argues that the First Amendment permits only regulation of the *how* and *where* of expression but not expression itself.
10. 390 U.S. 629, 638, 649-650 (1968).
11. See especially R. Kuh, *Foolish Figleaves: Pornography in and out of Court* (1967).
12. 397 U.S. 728, 736, 738 (1970).
13. *The New York Times,* August 5, 1973. Sec. D, page 11, col. 2.

II

ADMINISTRATIVE INNOVATIONS FOR THE COURTS

I. GAYLE SHUMAN and JOHN MOWEN

4. THE JURY SYSTEM: OLD PROBLEMS AND A NEW ALTERNATIVE

Depending upon one's attitude, the American jury represents either a bastion of democracy or a pit of prejudice. For five centuries it has remained fundamentally unchanged. During this time, history has witnessed the printing press, the industrial revolution, urbanization, the development of instantaneous communications, and the creation of a technological society. The fabric of modern society bears little resemblance to that of the fifteenth century. Yet, the jury system grinds on, set in its medieval ways. Two recent decisions by the Supreme Court, however, portend possible revolutionary changes. In a 1972 decision the Court stated that unanimity of a verdict is not required at the state level.[1] In 1970 the Court decided that a jury could be composed of fewer than twelve persons.[2] With the stage set for change, the atmosphere may now be conducive to the introduction of a newer, broader concept—the lay-jury.

The lay-juror system avoids the imperfections of the present system, yet retains its strengths. Our goal here is to present a brief digression into the history of the jury to indicate how it evolved as prelude to discussion of the lay-jury system.

The Jury's History

Early references to juries may be found in ancient Egyptian writings and Greek tragedies. Twelve citizens of Athens, called

I. Gayle Shuman is Director of the Center for Criminal Justice at Arizona State University, and John Mowen is a Research Associate at the same institution.

together by Athena, the patron goddess of wisdom, tried Orestes for the murder of his mother. Later in Athens, assemblies consisting of 200 to 1,500 citizens tried cases. The jurors voted in secret to decide both facts and law. The ancient Romans used from fifty-one to seventy-five judices who were chosen once a year to try cases.

How the jury began in the British Islands is uncertain. Probably the most accurate explanation is that the system now in use blended several influences, one of which was certainly the Frankish jury imported by William the Conqueror. Prior to 1066 A.D. the Angles and the Saxons possessed a governmental structure with some aspects bearing similarity to a jury system. For example, Edward the Confessor (1024–1066 A.D.) had parties settle boundary disputes by referring the matter to a group of neighbors sworn to find the truth.

In its development the jury competed against other contemporary methods of justice. The most infamous brand—the ordeals—took several forms. For example, the accused might have to pick a stone out of boiling water or walk barefooted over red-hot plowshares. If no blisters or infection appeared after three days, he was deemed innocent. Another test consisted of throwing the individual, thumbs tied to toes, into the water. The individual who sank was considered innocent, since the water would "reject" the guilty. (The luckless individual was retrieved from the water if he sank.)

The primitive forerunner of the jury system evolved both for the benefit of the common man and the English kings. Religious authorities had implemented the ordeals. Thus in a long-term struggle to wrest temporal power from the Church, the Crown desired a different method of determining guilt and innocence. Later, as the kings collected power, the system protected the English people from the capricious justice dispensed by judges working for the Crown.

The ancestors of the jury were indeed primitive: early in the system's development the jurors were witnesses rather than impartial outsiders, and could be punished for rendering false verdicts—a process called attaint. The jury was for a time composed entirely of lawyers. At other times efforts were made systematically to insert one's peers onto the jury. Thus if one were a foreign merchant, he would be tried before six foreign merchants and six honest townsmen. The number twelve was not sacred; anywhere from six to sixty-six jurors have been used.

The immediate roots of our present jury system are embedded in the Constitution of the United States. Article III states:

The trial of all crimes, except in cases of impeachment, shall be by jury; and such trial shall be held in the state where the said crimes shall have been committed; but when not committed within any state, the trial shall be at such place or places as the Congress may by Law have directed.

The Sixth Amendment outlines four additional provisions. The trial must be: "speedy," "public," in "the state and district" where the alleged crime occurred, and before an "impartial jury."

Despite the refinements of the Sixth Amendment, the concept remained couched in highly general terms. Specifics relating to the size of the jury, method of selection, unanimity of the verdict, and the conduct of the trial were drawn from Common Law. As has already been seen, the Common Law was far from uniform.

Five Problems with the Jury

The jury is an adaptive species. As the fabric, composition, and technical level of Anglo-Saxon society changed, so did the jury. Its evolution, however, has not kept pace with the rapid transition of our society. Increased urbanization, mobility, communication, technological level, and psychological expertise have undermined the ability of the jury to function in a manner envisioned by the writers of the Constitution.

Five major problem areas exist within the jury system. The first area concerns the average person's lack of expertise in the complicated task of being a competent juror. Ordinarily the juror knows little more about the trial situation than what he has seen on television. He knows essentially nothing about the fine points of the law and is unfamiliar with legal terminology. Within the foreign atmosphere of the trial situation his ability to glean the important from the unimportant diminishes. The late Federal Judge Jerome Frank stated:

The surroundings of inquiry during a jury trial differ extraordinarily from those in which the juryman conducts his ordinary affairs. At a trial, the jurors hear evidence in a public place, under conditions of a kind to which they are unaccustomed: No juror is able to withdraw to his own room, or office for private individual reflection. And at the close of the trial, the jurors are pressed for time in reaching their joint decision. Even twelve experienced judges, deliberating together, would probably not function well under the conditions we impose on the twelve inexperienced men.[3]

The typical juror also has difficulty following lengthy cases and determining how the law should be applied. In most states note taking is forbidden, placing an added strain on jurors' information-processing capabilities. Jurors are not allowed to probe witnesses, so their questions go unanswered, indeed unasked. In sum, one must draw a picture of twelve out-of-place individuals who attempt simultaneously to understand the foreign legal terminology, follow and remember a case without notes, adapt to the unfamiliar atmosphere of the courtroom, and arrive at a just decision without having their individual questions asked or answered. To make the morass worse, during the trial the juror will also be exposed to a flood of testimony from witnesses. James Marshall convincingly shows in *Law and Psychology in Conflict* that a naïve juror has an extremely difficult task in interpreting witness testimony.[4] Three distortions of eye-witness testimony can occur. The first is in the very perception of an event. Occurrences seen only briefly, under less than optimal circumstances, tend to be perceived within the individual's own frame of reference or expectations. Secondly, recollection dims. Often trials occur months or even years after the original incident. Over this period memories fade, the true order of recall is lost, newspaper accounts and the witnesses' attitudes bias jurors' recollections, and the lawyers' questioning replaces old memories with newer, more plausible ones. Thirdly, distortion occurs in the articulation of testimony. Difficulty arises in precisely verbalizing immediate occurrences. Delay exacerbates the problem. Just as attitudes can mold memories to fit a person's beliefs, words can take an unclear memory and alter its true content.

Marshall reported an experiment depicting the vagaries of recall which can plague eye-witnesses. Air Force personnel were asked to estimate the speed of a moving car. The guesses ranged from ten to fifty miles per hour for a car going twelve miles per hour.

The fact that juries place a high degree of reliance upon eye-witness testimony magnifies the problem of witness inaccuracies. Jurors themselves are eye-witnesses to the testimony, so the problems associated with witness testimony also apply to its interpretation. This compounding of errors seriously distorts the efficacy of jury deliberations.

The second major problem area of the jury trial concerns the unconscious prejudice affecting the jurors. Theoretically, the screening performed during "voir dire" excises those who seem prejudiced. (However, quite possibly some prejudiced individuals deliberately deny their attitude in order to serve on the jury.) The procedure of "voir dire" allows attorneys to eliminate jurors either "for cause" or "peremptorily." One can eliminate "for cause" those individuals who reveal obvious prejudices. A limited number of peremptory challenges permits a juror to be excused for any reason. Thus, talented lawyers with knowledge of appropriate techniques for identifying those who might possess unconscious prejudice may influence the outcome of a case by selecting a jury composed of individuals with biases favorable to their clients.

One can identify two types of unconscious prejudice affecting a jury. The first, one might call circumstantial. This type includes attitudes formed by pretrial publicity or by the accused being charged with a crime. Pretrial publicity is particularly insidious. Such publicity seriously alters the ability of jurors to maintain open minds when reaching a decision.

The second type of prejudice is of a psychological nature. Each person tends to view the world in a particular idiosyncratic manner. The person may be totally unaware of the biases which can result from his or her personality make-up. In trial situations two methods have been identified to make illicit use of such unconscious prejudices. The first uses a sociological approach. One cannot give a battery of personality tests to each individual juror under the present system of selection. Thus, in order to exploit biases, one has to use information easily obtained. By polling the community on questions pertinent to a trial, one can obtain a statistical analysis of what demographic characteristics (such as sex, education, age, occupation, etc.) an individual favorable to a client should possess.

In the trial of the Harrisburg Seven, such a technique was used with apparent success to pack a jury with individuals favorably disposed to the defendants. In this case seven people (three priests, a nun, an ex-priest, an ex-nun, and a Pakistani) were tried for conspiring to raid draft boards, kidnap Henry Kissinger, and blow up heating tunnels in Washington. In order to avoid a mistrial, the Federal trial judge allowed the defense twenty-eight peremptory challenges. Research performed in the Harrisburg area indicated that the ideal defense juror should be

A female Democrat with no religious preference and a white-collar job or a skilled blue-collar job. Further, a "good" defense juror would "sympathize" with some elements of the defendant's views regarding the Vietnam war, at least tolerate the rights of citizens to resist governmental policies non-violently, and give signs that he or she would presume the defendants to be innocent until proven guilty.[5]

Defense counsel were able to select seven individuals rated as "good." Six of the jurors rated as "best" were challenged by the prosecution, who came to similar conclusions. The five remaining jurors turned out to be rated as "maybes" by the defense. In retrospect, it is impossible to state unequivocally that the jury-packing procedure affected the verdict. While the defendants were found guilty of illegally passing letters out of the prison, the jury was deadlocked on the other charges. It seems plausible that the complicated, highly ambiguous case may well have turned out differently without those efforts.

The use of these sociological techniques to select favorable juries has won other adherents. The attorneys of John Mitchell and Maurice Stans employed social-scientist analysts to construct a jury profile. Similar profiles were used in the trial of the participants in the takeover at Wounded Knee, South Dakota. Expense limits the use of the procedure. Only the rich or those involved in controversial causes have the money available to finance the necessary research. Uneven justice, more favorable to the rich, may well result.

The other method of obtaining a favorable jury makes a more direct use of psychological techniques. Individuals possess personality characteristics which predispose them to view the world in a particular way. One such bias possessed by almost everyone is the tendency to attribute better motives to those who are good-looking than to those who are less well blessed. Research has indicated that a beautiful woman will be given a lighter sentence than an unattractive woman receives, as long as the crime committed does not involve the deceitful use of her attractiveness.

A more sinister personality characteristic is the dimension of authoritarianism. Individuals may be classified from highly authoritarian to nonauthoritarian. The extreme authoritarian reveres those who possess power, follows unflinchingly their desires, is politically conservative, and tends to be more lenient to an authority figure. He tends to be particularly harsh on minorities and those who are different from him. At the other extreme is the nonauthoritarian. He hates authority figures on trial, while being more lenient toward minorities and the "underdog." Incisive and shrewd questioning allows lawyers to reject jurors revealing personality characteristics damaging to their client's interests.

Biases may have a large effect on a verdict. Juries generally receive close, difficult cases. As the ambiguity of the evidence increases, so does the impact of circumstantial and psychological prejudices. Further, the influence of highly persuasive jurors increases. If such individuals are biased, the verdict, reached through communication and persuasion, may be seriously distorted.

Another source of unconscious prejudice occurs in the courtroom itself. During the heat of the trial, each lawyer attempts to swing the emotions of the jury to his side. Pain and anguish are described vividly. Jurors are reminded of the axiom, "There but for the grace of God go I"—implying that they should not judge too harshly for fear of the same calamity afflicting them. A humorous quote tells something about the lawyers and the jury trial:

Gambling on what a jury will do is like playing the horses. The notorious undependability of juries, the chance involved is one of the absorbing features of the law. That's what makes the practice of law, like prostitution, one of the last of the unpreditable professions—both employ the seductive arts, both try to display their wares to the best advantage, and both must pretend to woo total strangers. And that's why most successful trial lawyers are helpless showmen; that's why they are about nine-tenths ham actor and one-tenth lawyer.[6]

The first two problems with the jury system concerned the jurors' lack of expertise and the unconscious prejudices which may influence its decision. Each problem has been magnified by our technological society. The scientific analysis of evidence is incomprehensible to many laymen. Cases sometimes involve problems nonexistent thirty years ago. Invasion of privacy, computer crimes, hijacking, and many civil suits are examples. Mass communication, particularly television, was not present. Psychological and sociological techniques were still in their infancy, confined largely to the ivory towers of the universities. Demands placed on the juror today are far more severe than at any time in the past.

In a case vividly depicting how a jury can totally ignore scientific evidence, Charlie Chaplin was accused of fathering an illegitimate child. Blood tests indicated his innocence; the jury concluded otherwise. What was responsible for the verdict? Perhaps Chaplin's wealth had an impact. Perhaps an imagined facial resemblance to the child prompted the decision. Whatever the reasons, it indicates a distrust in, if not incomprehension of, conclusive scientific evidence.

Our changing society has added a third difficulty with the current jury system. With increased urbanization and transportation, the jury is becoming less and less a jury of one's peers.

The young, the poor, minorities and blue-collar workers, are underrepresented on jury rolls. Within a large urban area, several separate cultures co-exist with moral standards dissimilar from each other and from the larger population. With the present system an individual is usually tried outside his familiar neighborhood by faceless strangers possibly of another culture. A jury of one's peers is an illusion.

The fourth problem involves the lengthy delays in trials. An inverse relation exists between the delay of a trial and the quality of justice. The twelve-man jury is one important factor in causing the long delays. The selection of the jury, the need for detailed instructions by the judge, and the lawyers' pandering to the jury all contribute to delay.

The fifth problem with the jury concerns the general verdict. A jury determines facts and theoretically arrives at a verdict based upon such facts. When the foreman reports the verdict, however, he does not detail how the jury viewed the facts. He merely states in general terms, "We find for the plaintiff for X amount" or "We find for the defendant." "The general verdict serves as the great procedural opiate. . . . (It) draws the curtain upon human errors, and soothes us with assurance that we have obtained the unattainable."[7]

The Strengths of the Jury

As the preceding paragraphs indicate, the American jury suffers from old age. But despite lameness, myopia, and lack of sophistication, it still possesses fundamental strengths. Its apolitical nature is its greatest asset. Verdicts are rarely corrupted because of the impossibility of predicting which trial a potential juror will witness. Prosecutors and judges can also act against the public's interest. The Supreme Court noted that the function of the jury in the modern society is to prevent governmental oppression by providing a "safeguard against the corrupt or over-zealous prosecutor and against the compliant, biased or eccentric judge."[8]

Other strengths emerge when comparisons are made to the

alternative system most often proposed—the judge. Countries throughout the world use a judge without a jury. But problems exist in this system also. A judge may be a highly political figure working for interests not necessarily coinciding with those of justice. His higher public exposure creates greater risks of attempts to influence him. When difficult, unpopular decisions must be made, justice may suffer for fear of his job or his safety. Further, deliberations by a judge alone lack the helpful interaction between individuals where each person's knowledge and opinions are considered. Implicit in a democracy is the concept that better decisions come from a collection of individuals than from a single person.

An Alternative System

The proposed lay-juror system presented below retains the strengths of the American jury but avoids the above five shortcomings. It retains broad rights to a fair trial by jury as guaranteed in the Constitution. Where it recommends new techniques of selecting jurors or advocates changes in trial procedure, it is to correct deficiencies in the current system. The lay-jury proposal integrates modifications into a coherent system which has promise of reducing the uneven dispensing of justice inherent in the American jury.

The lay-jury system differs from the American jury in several key respects. Currently when an individual receives notice for jury duty, he must be available for a period of months. In the lay-juror system an individual will become a full-time, salaried, juror for a period of three years. In order to be eligible he must perform acceptably on a battery of personality and intelligence tests. The personality tests will be given in order to identify individuals less prone to the types of unconscious prejudice previously presented. The intelligence tests will insure that the individuals selected have the ability to reason and understand testimony. The purpose will *not* be to select the highly intelligent, but rather to avoid those incapable of making rational decisions in the complicated atmosphere of the courtroom.

The usual procedure of selecting jurors consists of randomly choosing individuals from voter registration rolls. Lay-jurors will be volunteers who, in addition to meeting the intellectual and personality prerequisites, fit certain demographic characteristics which insure a jury representative of the population. To adequately represent the population characteristics of the area, the following procedure can be used: An analysis of the population characteristics of the particular urban area would first occur. Ethnic, age, sex, and wealth variables would be included. Next, the average number and frequency of jury trials conducted in the area's courts system would be ascertained. From this would be derived the number of individuals necessary to make up the lay-jury pool. After determining the number required, the population characteristics would be matched to the jury panel size. Thus, for a city such as Phoenix, Arizona, for each one hundred people on the jury panel there might be positions for four Blacks, fifteen Mexican-Americans, two Indians, and seventy-nine Whites. Other stratifications would be for sex, age, and socio-economic bracket. From the lay-jury pool names would be drawn at random before a trial, so the same people would not sit together for each case.

In most localities an elected jury commissioner, rather than a political appointee, is in charge of selecting the jurors. A similar procedure would apply to the lay-juror system. It is particularly important that the jury selection be totally free of political harassment so that jurors can be chosen in a clinical manner.

One unfounded criticism of the stratified sampling technique of obtaining the lay-jurors is that the poor, the religiously unorthodox, the uneducated, and minorities might be excluded from or at least underrepresented in the lay-juror pool. For several reasons this concern is minor. The first is that the stratified sample will include specific positions for those of various minority races, those who are poor, and those with less than a high-school education. (The ability to read, write, and reason effectively must be possessed, however.) Second, the religiously unorthodox will have essentially the same chance of being represented in the lay-juror pool as any other group of people. Of course, because all lay-jurors voluntarily apply for the job, there may be variations in representation because a particular group, not included in the stratifications, would decline to volunteer. Most groups, however, are likely to be adequately represented.

Jurors now receive little training in how to perform their complicated task; lay-jurors would be given training in trial proceedings, legal terminology, evaluation of witness testimony, and determination of a verdict. With this added information, consistency in reaching verdicts would increase, with a corresponding improvement in the quality of justice.

The size of a jury in most states is twelve, particularly in criminal cases. The lay-jury will be composed of six individuals. The debate on the relative merits of six versus twelve-man juries remains unsettled, but the cost savings of six rather than twelve is substantial. Because no difference between the two alternatives in dispensing justice has been demonstrated, economic considerations favor six-man juries.

Rules regarding the presentation of evidence are currently rigid. For example, hearsay is not allowed. Hearsay is a kind of second-hand evidence where a witness relates a statement made by another individual who cannot be cross-examined. The present hearsay rule renders valuable evidence lost. Because the overall competency of the lay-jurors will be significantly improved over that of today's jurors, the need for excluding hearsay and other similar evidence is greatly reduced. Also forbidden from testimony is past information about lawyer's fees, income taxes, and insurance. In the present system the jurors are left to speculate on these factors. Such speculation leads to wide variations in verdicts even though similar evidence is often presented. For a lay-jury, such evidence could be freely brought out with less fear of misuse.

Currently "voir dire" is a time-consuming task often misused by lawyers. In the lay-jury system many of the reasons for conducting "voir dire" would be removed. The individuals in the jury pool would be chosen for their lack of prejudice. "Voir dire" would be performed by the judge and limited to a few questions directly relevant to the case. For example, if the case involved a serious automobile accident, questions could be asked about previous experiences with such tragedies. Other questions would be: (1) do you know or are you related to the accused, and (2) do you have any potential prejudices which could conceivably influence your verdict? This change in questioning will substantially speed-up jury selection.

Jurors now have no way of having their questions answered. In many states, no notes may be taken. Under the lay-jury system the foreman of the jury (selected randomly each trial from among the six lay-jurors) would have the right, after each witness is heard, to pass questions to the judge for him to ask the witness. Jurors would also be allowed to take notes.

As mentioned previously, jurors now must only give a general verdict. Under the lay-juror system, the foreman of the jury would present to the judge the jury's findings of facts and all relevant data used to arrive at the decision.

The Strengths of the Lay-Jury

The strengths of the lay-jury come from two sources. The first lies in its foundation—the current American jury and its heritage. The lay-jury retains the features of our present system which have made it successful for so long. The second source of strength comes from its innovations.

One important innovation is the juror's three-year term of service. By obtaining juror longevity, an efficient and thorough selection process is possible. Time will be available for the administration of personality inventories and tests of reasoning skills. Such empirically-derived and validated psychological scales do exist. With adaptation and further testing they have promise of insuring that the lay-jurors will be relatively free of prejudice.

In addition, the long retention period enables the development of a training program. Training insures that lay-jurors will understand applicable law, be accustomed to the trial setting, discern the important from the irrelevant, and be aware of the distortions in witness testimony. Further, the training will include ways to avoid biasing, circumstantial prejudice, and should inoculate jurors against the emotionalism which lawyers attempt to generate.

Reaching a decision in a court of law is a complex task requiring training and sufficient time on the job to first develop the necessary skills and then apply them. The realities of the current situation demand emphasis on selection and training. The present high juror turn-over rate, however, makes such an investment prohibitively expensive. Thus, for economic reasons juror longevity is essential.

Another innovation and strength of the lay-jury is the method of providing a pool of jurors more closely representative of the population than the current system. By systematically sampling from the population (to include the young and the racial minorities, who represent a large proportion of defendants in criminal cases), the problems inherent in the use of voter registration rolls are reduced.

Two features of the lay-jury should reduce court delays. The first involves the changes in the procedure of "voir dire." The second encompasses the atmosphere which the lay-jury should create in the courtroom. Currently the atmosphere is one of emotionalism where lawyers employ time-consuming dramatics and orations. With the lay-jury the need for courtroom antics will be reduced. Lawyers will find it necessary to present well-prepared and researched cases to the trained lay-jury.

A fourth innovation of the lay-jury involves an improvement in the procedure of rendering a decision. The foreman would present to the judge not only the general verdict but also the determination of facts upon which the decision was reached. Such a procedure will allow judicial review and will focus the jurors' attention on the facts and away from individual biases. It will also inhibit jurors from failing to convict because they believe the relevant law to be bad. At the time of the American Revolution the right of the jury to make law was generally recognized. With the Constitution, however, the reason to have juries as lawmakers disappeared. Americans no longer need to be protected from corrupt judges working for the King of England. A jury's refusal to convict because of what it considers a bad law means that justice is dispensed in a capricious, uncertain manner. The lay-jury system should inhibit verdicts based on factors other than the evidence.

Some Possible Problems

At the theoretical level the proposed lay-juror system improves upon the shortcomings of the jury system used today. Further, it avoids the problems inherent in systems using only a single judge. Several practical questions, however, must be dealt with before implementing the system. Is it constitutional? Would the American public accept and have confidence in it? Is it practical in terms of finding acceptable volunteers and in terms of cost?

A strong argument can be made that such a system is constitutional. As stated previously, the provisions for a jury are couched in broad terms within the Constitution and Common Law. The historical interpretation states that the jury must have three features: "(1) There must be twelve jurors, neither more nor less; (2) The trial must be conducted in the presence and under the supervision of a judge to instruct the jury concerning the law; and (3) The verdict must be unanimous."[9] The first and third features, however, were not clear-cut either under Common Law or the Constitution, and recently the Supreme Court has ruled that neither unanimity nor twelve jurors is necessary. The second feature is retained in the lay-juror system.

The Fourteenth Amendment applies the constitutional provisions to the states. The applicable portion states that

No state shall make or enforce any law which shall abridge the privileges or immunities of citizens of the United States; nor shall any State deprive any person of life, liberty, or property without due process of law; nor deny to any person within its jurisdiction the equal protection of the laws.

The question then becomes: Would the lay-jury abridge privileges or immunities, deny due process, or deny equal protection under the laws? As already indicated, no particular concept in the lay-jury system specifically violates the rights above. Two concepts, however, have not undergone the Supreme Court's analysis. The first involves the extensive use of personality tests to select jurors. Inevitably some individuals fail to meet criteria set for competency. Rather than a fault in the system, this aspect is a strength. Minimum standards of competency are set for most technical occupations. Juries should have them also. As to using psychological tests to set such minimum standards, the *Yale Law Journal* has advocated their use, as well as indicating that in the Supreme Court decision of Glasser v. United States, minimum standards for juries were deemed necessary.[10] The second aspect of the lay-jury not to undergo Supreme Court scrutiny involves the juror's three-year term of service. The substantial investment in training lay-jurors demands that they have sufficient longevity to acquire and apply their expertise. Thus even though the lay-jury employs concepts new to the American jury system, the constitutional rights of the public should not be violated. Indeed, because of the innovative changes recommended, one can foresee the time when these rights are given increased protection.

Will the public have confidence in the lay-jury system? Only by subjecting it to public scrutiny and criticism can a determination be made of the confidence which citizens would have in such a system. For two overriding reasons it should promote confidence. First, it allows citizens to be tried by qualified individuals representative of the population. A second, more pragmatic reason is that jury duty is now an inconvenience. The lay-jury system will remove the uncertainty of whether an individual will be called away from his job or home, and avoid the financial losses sometimes incurred by jury service.

The questions which present the most formidable problems concern the system's cost and whether sufficient qualified individuals will apply for positions. Both of these topics require in-depth studies which should occur after the theoretical underpinnings have been thoroughly discussed.

The lay-jury makes basic and needed changes in the American jury system. Yet, it does *not* depart from the concepts guaranteed by the Constitution. It is a continuation of the evolution of the jury. It will breathe life into the American judicial system by applying the modern medicine of scientifically-validated personality tests and proven survey methods. In short, the lay-jury is a system whose merits deserve debate, research, and study.

NOTES

1. Apodaca v. Oregon, 406 U.S. 404 (1972).
2. Williams v. Florida, 399 U.S. 78 (1970).
3. Jerome Frank, *Courts on Trial, Myth and Reality in American Justice* (New York: Atheneum Publishers, 1963), pp. 119–20.
4. James Marshall, *Law and Psychology in Conflict* (New York: Doubleday & Company, Inc., 1969).
5. Jay Schulman et al., "Recipe for a Jury," *Psychology Today* (May 1973), p. 40.
6. Marcus Gleisser, *Juries and Justice* (New Jersey: A. S. Barnes & Co., 1968), p. 243.
7. Frank, *Courts on Trial*, p. 114.
8. Duncan v. Louisiana, 391 U.S. 145, 88 S. Ct. 1444, 29 L. Ed. 2d 491 (1968).
9. Edward Dumbald, *The Constitution of the United States* (Oklahoma: University of Oklahoma Press, 1964), p. 369.
10. "Psychological Tests and Standards of Competence for Selecting Jurors," 65 *Yale Law Journal* (1956), pp. 531–42.

PATRICK D. McANANY

5. RECOMMENDATIONS FOR IMPROVING THE AILING PROBATION SYSTEM

In 1970 to 1971, I was project director for a major effort to draft reform legislation dealing with postadjudicatory matters in Illinois. It was agreed among staff, advisors, and the sponsoring legislative commission that probation was the most significant element of our efforts. But several things happened to this consensus on the way to legislation.

In the first place, the subcommittee on probation bogged down with a plethora of suggested models for organizing probation services. After much debate, the "safe" path was chosen to leave probation departments under court control. After a great deal of debate and soul searching this suggestion was drafted into the Code and duly presented to the legislature. Without pausing to discuss other issues, the committee of legislators unceremoniously hacked the probation services section from the Code as "too radical." They, too, considered probation as central to the Code—but they wanted it the way it had always been, underused and overtalked. The Code, miraculously, is in effect today, with everything up to date except the vital center of the whole effort. (*Illinois Unified Code of Corrections, with Commentary*, West, 1972.)

Today, there are increasing numbers of voices which recognize the centrality of probation to a rational scheme of criminal justice. Among the more authoritative, the National Advisory Commission on Criminal Justice Standards and Goals has added

Patrick D. McAnany is Associate Professor of Criminal Justice, University of Illinois (Chicago Circle) and chief draftsman of the Illinois corrections code.

its voice to the call for recognition and reform of probation. Unfortunately, the Commission's recommendations may be taken seriously and become normative to a great deal of legislative reform. The thrust of these recommendations is basically at odds with an eminently healthy development in probation over the past few years. What, in essence, the Commission suggests is that probation and all other correctional programs be consolidated into a single, monolithic state agency. Whatever the wisdom of this conglomerative urge for other correctional programs, as to probation, at least, it is at odds with common sense and with many of the other good recommendations that the Commission makes.

This chapter will look at the past decade of probation to illuminate where it stands today. This will give us some sense of the direction in which probation can and should move in order to preserve and strengthen its hard-earned values. Among these we will look at the "due processification" that has overtaken probation, its evolution as the heart of community-based corrections, and the role that the community should play in its operation. Finally, we will examine the argument the Commission puts forward for the subsumption of probation into a massive, unified state agency.

A Due Process Evolution: From Mercy to Justice

If one looks at probation as an activity of the sentencing jurisdiction of the court, as indeed probation requires, it is evident that a major evolution has taken place from the time of John Augustus. Probation as exercised in Boston in 1841 was an exercise of the court's inherent criminal equity powers. In certain cases, however, justice requires that the law be applied not by the letter but the spirit. Thus, the court in Boston chose in sentencing some first offenders to suspend the imposition of sentence and commit them to the custody of Augustus. There was no statutory or rule authority for this, but the equities of the situation called for the judge to exercise what obviously was an extraordinary jurisdiction. While few judges are inclined to openly set aside the legal sentence, all will admit that they have contrived to accomplish this end in one way or another to achieve justice. The Boston judge was only making explicit what was inherent—an obligation to do justice. Specifically, what Augustus wanted and what the judge ordered was a suspension of the sentence of incarceration and a release of the convicted offender to the custody of Augustus.

The next step in the evolution came when the practice of probation grew. People began to question the power of the courts to do equity and avoid law. Litigation put the issue as a constitutional conflict in separation of powers. The courts, it was argued, were in reality exercising clemency powers reserved to the chief executive alone. This argument overlooked the fact that suspension of sentence and conditional release were markedly different from pardon, but it was played against a judiciary that hesitated to assert an extraordinary jurisdictional power in what was fast becoming a common practice. Probation had by its very success brought the issue to a head.

Since the legislature fixed the penalty of incarceration which probation was intended to avoid, it was considered the proper agency to provide for the conditional withdrawal of its enforcement against certain convicted offenders. Probation got its first major impetus when legislatures began to authorize courts to suspend the imposition of incarceration and release the convicted person to the community under specific conditions. Even with this step probation remained an extraordinary alternative restricted in use to only certain crimes and criminals, notably first offenders for minor offenses. Further, probation was not a sentence but a suspension of the "real" sentence, incarceration. No appeal lay from an order of probation and no law governed the exercise of this jurisdiction of benevolence.

This status of probation was the accepted version until quite recently. Certain changes were gradually added by more liberal jurisdictions. Restrictions on the use of probation for most crimes were relaxed. Probation became appealable. Certain conditions of probation were challenged as unconstitutional. But while probation became the major sentencing alternative to incarceration, it remained a suspension of the lawful or "real" sentence and was considered within the absolute discretion of the sentencing court.

The next major step was taken when probation was changed from a substitution for sentence to one of several sentencing alternatives, just as fines had traditionally been for misdemeanors where courts did not wish to impose a jail sentence. While this change of status has not yet been broadly adopted, its meaning has been anticipated by several Supreme Court cases where probationary status received the due process consideration of sentencing.[1] Clearly the status of probation as a sentence makes the arguments that much more forceful. All of the due process rights that sentencing has come to entail cannot be denied to probation merely because it is a suspension of sentence rather than the "real thing." Probation becomes, with this step in the process, no longer a jurisdiction of mercy but one of justice.

The final link in the evolution is just now underway. Although the American Law Institute had early recommended that probation be considered not only a full sentencing alternative with incarceration, but the normative or preferred one, no state or federal jurisdiction adopted this radical model. But this suggestion was incorporated into the authoritative American Bar Association's Minimum Standards of 1970 and 1973. This preferred position of probation has been extended even further by the National Advisory Commission on Criminal Justice Standards and Goals. It states the proposition in terms of "least restrictive alternative," putting incarceration as the most extreme measure requiring the most justification from the facts.

But even in its more modest form, as set out in the *Model Penal Code*, probation as the preferred sentence reverses the traditional position of probation, which for so many years had to be justified by extreme cases of hardship or injustice. As one reflects on the evolutionary process, it seems clear that one of the motive forces was the growing realization that prisons and jails were shockingly inhumane frauds on the public and on offenders. Thus probation appeared to be the only alternative for sane judges who wished to do justice, quite apart from their inclination to give mercy.

The implications of this evolution for probation have not all been worked out. At the procedural level some things are becoming clear. For instance, even prior to probation becoming a sentence, a number of court decisions began the due processification of probation.

As a first recognition of rights in the offender to probation, the Supreme Court accorded revocation of probation and resentencing the status of a critical stage at which counsel must be present.[2] Further, a hearing was mandated at which the charge had to be determined on the basis of evidence produced in open court with opportunity of confrontation and cross-examination.[3] A review of denial of probation in most jurisdictions was possible.[4] This included the challenge to legislative restrictions placed on the initial grant of probation;[5] the right to present and have the court consider evidence favorable to probation;[6] and the right of access to presentence reports considered by the judge in sentencing.[7] These cases point toward a due process status for probation as a part of the general sentencing power.

The substantive implications of this due process evolution are much less clear and tentative. Probation had begun and developed as a dual entity. It was *mercy* exercised by the court for purposes of *rehabilitation.* Indeed, as the negative factors of prison became clearer, the reason it was advanced so strongly as an alternative was its rehabilitative superiority. Nearly all the official literature stressed this fact. Probation was a natural captive for the medical model of correctional philosophy. Probation officers became "psychological experts" and probationers became their "patients."

The time seems appropriate now to question whether probation can be a full sentencing alternative with incarceration and fines, without fulfilling the more demanding and complex role of criminal sanctions generally. Probation, in a way, is on a similar footing with juvenile corrections. As long as the court's jurisdiction is seen as an act of mercy or leniency and not justice, then the justifying theme of rehabilitation *alone* is acceptable. But once justice becomes part of the picture, rehabilitation by itself is insufficient and self-defeating. This same attack has been made, and tellingly so, on the official rhetoric of prisons. If rehabilitation is the only or primary goal of prisons, then not only has it been mocked in practice, but it has also been used to conceal a plan of punishment that selects trouble makers for "therapy" that is political in nature and brutalizing in effect. The issue has been raised about the reconcilability of due process with any rehabilitative regimen not totally voluntary in nature.

The major problem for probation is that for so long it has been viewed from the perspective of mercy-rehabilitation only. The reason a judge placed people on probation, according to the official rhetoric, was to rehabilitate them. If probation now becomes a full sentencing alternative in which justice as well as rehabilitation are conjoined, then we have to see things differently. This is not the time or place to elaborate a full philosophy for probation, but several points may contribute to this future task. For one thing, probation has the primary goal of protection of the public. While this was often explained in terms of the rehabilitation of the individual, in practical terms it was enforced by a surveillance/revocation practice which looked carefully at new criminal activity. For another, probation may have been regarded as a break for the offender—as indeed it was, viewed against the rigors of prison—but in reality conditional release could be coercive in the extreme. Intensive supervision might mean anything from daily reporting to submitting to body searches at any hour. Probation is itself punitive. How the conflicting goals of rehabilitation, deterrence, retribution, and incapacitation can be reconciled in theory or practice remains a major problem for criminal justice generally. Probation has been able to sidestep this knotty problem by insisting it was an act of mercy not subject to due process scrutiny. But that day is over. Probation now has to work through an understanding of itself as a jurisdiction of justice.

The Evolution of Probation: From Reform to Reintegration

As probation was the first expression of hostility to the conception and practice of incarceration, so diversion has become the most recent. The question is whether probation, parole, diversion, and all the other minor variations on this theme have a positive side, or whether they are based solely on the deficiencies of prisons. The answer is problematic; prison itself was created as the humane alternative to prior punishments. If asked to state the current justifying philosophy for all of these correctional developments, one would say: reintegration.

The philosophic core of probation has been humanitarian. Taking the harsh concept of punishment, it has turned its deterrence doctrine inside out and insisted that the best protection of the public from criminals is the rehabilitation of criminals. Instead of punishing criminals, which is wasteful, we should rehabilitate them, which is not only a more effective means of protecting society, but more humanitarian as well.

Beginning with the advent of probation in Boston in 1841, its justification was this humanitarian appeal, coupled with the argument that it worked better than prison in protecting society. In its early days, the rehabilitation philosophy was expressed in terms of moral reform, as that was the conception of what had generated crime in the individual's life: a failure of morals. Later, this came to be displaced by the more familiar medical model.

For probation this change in underlying justification required a shift in role for the person who administered probation to the offender. From the morally earnest citizen who could set the erring sinner on the straight and narrow path, probation moved to the professional, trained in psychiatric social work, who could counsel the emotionally disturbed patient. This latter role predominated in professional literature until the last decade; it still underlies the common conception of probation in practice. This notion of probation as rehabilitative therapy dependent on the expert has suffered erosion by development of a due process of justice model for probation.

Probation currently explains its work as reintegration of the offender into the community. This philosophy implies a theory for criminogenesis, as did the former ones. Crime as sin or sickness seems less convincing than the environmental approach. Crime seems to be generated from the failures of the social milieu to provide individuals with proper ties to socializing influences such as the family, friends, schools, and employment. Whether, as in the case of the poor, this deficiency is explained as due to poverty, or to other causes, the results are the same. Youth who fail to find a stake in society through legitimate outlets seek and find rewards in illegal activity.

The resulting correctional treatment that derives from this analysis is called reintegration. Briefly, reintegration insists that corrections must adjust the institutions of society, not merely the individual offender. It is a failure of institutions that is the partial but crucial factor in crime. From this it follows that correction can only take place in the community where those institutions exist. Offenders cannot be corrected while locked up in prisons which exclude society. The community is the reality-setting where the offender must make it legitimately, coping with his own shortcomings and with the institutions that had short-changed him before. Reintegration has thus come to be expressed in the popular term of "community-based corrections."

The role of the probation officer now becomes one of community service brokerage. He helps tie the convict back into the community by seeking appropriate community resources to reintegrate him into the stabilizing social institutions of family, employment, education, career, and church. Where these services are not available or are carefully guarded against social undesirables, the probation officer assumes the role of advocate, persuading the community to change.

The role of the offender becomes more active and cooperative. Probation as reintegration suggests that the community rather than the offender, or at least mutually with him, has failed. Under this approach to crime, part or all the blame can be placed outside the offender to allow him to assume a more objective analysis of his career. Then, too, the probation officer is no longer the expert who understands the inner workings of the offender's mind; rather, he becomes a coordinator of needed social services, such as employment or housing, tasks which are much more manipulable than psychological motives. Finally, the offender under sentence is also a person with rights that must be respected.

A third element, left out of the earlier correctional philosophies, is the community. Reintegration makes the community central to its approach. Not only is the community the indispensable site of the new corrections; it is also part of the problem. Here, the success of the theory seems to dissipate. While it always was hard to achieve rehabilitation in actual cases, the theory of the medical model was tight and scientific. But when propounders of community-based corrections come to explaining how the community functions in their theory, the theory gets mushy and ambiguous.

The Ambivalent Community

Several things seem to be wrong with giving the community a role in probation. In the first place, the community has traditionally been viewed as the repository of a vengeful theory of justice. Secondly, the community is undefined, amorphous, and amateur when it comes to crime. Who is the community and what do they know about corrections? Finally, the community is conceived as the aggressor in any hardline analysis of reintegration. This will hardly serve a helpful purpose when reintegration also insists on the community providing services for people it fears—the offenders. But, whatever the problems, the community in "community-based corrections" cannot be eliminated. Logic demands its consideration.

Probation, more so than other correctional programs, has been willing to deal with the community. Probation is the first and most successful of the community-based programs. It has retained organizational ties with the communities through the local courts. In many places it has remained a community-controlled program as well. It has been the most successful in recruiting volunteers from the community to serve in a one-to-one capacity with offenders. It has clearly had appeal to the community sense of economy when its bills are compared with the high costs of prisons and jails.

Withal, probation still has not faced the difficulties propounded above. The due process model evolved by the courts suggests, however, that probation as a sentence of justice need not hide from the public as mere leniency. What probation officers and offenders know for a fact, that probation is a coercive status, should come to light for the general public. As part of the local community, probation must be responsive to the demands of the community for protection not by recommending fewer offenders for probation but by allowing citizen input about probation at the neighborhood level. If local determination in issues of social welfare, schools, and other matters is a growing trend, then criminal justice should be no exception. Probation as the correctional program that brings offenders back into the community immediately after conviction will suffer great pressures to deal with community ideas about protection. It is hardly a legitimate answer to the long divorce between the public and criminal justice to say that the public is benighted and bloodthirsty. In the name of the public, many inhumane and unjust things have been done over the past years to offenders. It is time that the public, whose name is so often invoked by officials without any semblance of accountability to it, be invited to speak for themselves.

This will not be easily carried out. For one thing, the public is not organized except along the broadest political-geographical lines. It has not been invited, except by a coaxing press, to express its views on crime. It has not had to wrestle with both sides of the question. To date, it has only had to worry about protecting itself against criminals and condemning crime. In a realistic setting, it will have to be concerned about issues of justice as well as social defense.

While certain moves have been made to get the public involved in corrections and criminal justice generally, new approaches are obviously called for where the public is asked to pay the bills *and* live with the convicted offenders, as implied in community-based corrections. One such approach might be to conceive the community along neighborhood lines responding roughly to areas of crime density. Such neighborhoods have some obvious reasons to be drawn together. Neighborhood councils, tried in the past with delinquency prevention, have not been very successful. They often were merely a reflection of the weak and disorganized state of the crimebreeding neighborhood. Here, however, the community would have a less demanding social role since it would be dealing with crime after the fact in a contained setting of probation.

Whatever the nature of the input, the community will have to share in the solution of the ultimate question: how dangerous will this convicted offender be in the community? Insofar as it is reflective of this input, probation will be successful in its reintegration role.

The final issue concerning the community is its criminogenic nature. If neighborhoods are crimebreeding, then a reintegration of the offender into them will result in continued failures. Here probation is called to its most fundamental task. To operate as a change-agent for social conditions endemic in certain neighborhoods is one thing. To attack systemwide maladjustments that run to the total community and beyond is quite another. Perhaps the best that probation could hope to do here is create, or cooperate in creating, community groups whose political goal is self-determination. If groups of poor neighbors can discern injustices attributable to the system, then groups of middle-class neighbors might also be able to come to similar insights. It will then become a matter of public articulation of these common issues in the political forum, where change will ultimately come.

Probation theory should be aware of another group needing self-determination in this process, namely, the offenders. If one conceives of the process of reintegration as a negotiation between the community, the court, and the offender, then obviously the offender needs to be let in on the process. To date, the offender has been represented by others. His attorney knows he is out of his depth when it comes to corrections; rarely does he do more than attack the issue of dangerousness by offering self-serving testimony of family members when seeking probation for his client. The probation officer is in an anomalous position since he is supposed to represent the court and the community as well as the offender. Obviously the court is aware of its divided loyalties in the decision to place a convicted person on probation.

Today, there is present and growing a movement among convicted offenders to organize themselves. While the movement has reflected greater activity among the prisonized offender, it has strong ties in the community where parolees and other ex-offenders confront the serious problems of reentry. It seems that an obvious negotiating element between the community, the individual offender, and the courts would be local groups of ex-offenders. Not that they would become the designated agent for the individual offender, to his exclusion; rather these groups could serve the very useful function of articulating offenders' point of view generally and providing street expertise that the negotiations might otherwise lack. While probation, like any correctional program, should ultimately be determined by the individual involved, a broadening of offender perspective by self-help groups such as these might be helpful in the extreme.

The Next Decade: Why the Commission on Standards and Goals Is Wrong

Obviously probation has some real problems left for it. As pointed out at the beginning of this chapter, probation appears to be a well-qualified heir to an evolution that has brought corrections back into the community. Yet probation has continued to struggle along under traditional views that ignore the fait accompli of the past decade.

To this situation the National Commission on Standards and Goals brings a great deal of light in its series of reports, especially on corrections (National Advisory Commission on Criminal Justice Standards and Goals, *Corrections,* January 1973). The problem with its view of probation is that it is self-contradictory, and one fears that the wrong side of the contradiction will be followed because it seems not only the more plausible, but much easier of accomplishment. On the one hand, the Commission recognizes the need for probation to be the centerpiece in its plan for community-based corrections; on the other, it recommends taking probation both out of the local courts and out of the local community by insisting that it become a wing of a gigantic and amorphous unified state correctional agency. The wrongheadedness of this latter recommendation needs examination.

First, the Commission makes the argument, familiar to many, why the courts are not suitable places for probation departments. In essence, the argument says that probation is a correctional program and courts are adjudicatory, not correctional agencies. Besides, courts are notably weak administratively, so probation suffers because the judge does not administer. This argument has some weight. Some states have successfully moved probation into the executive branch. Unfortunately, this issue is not the real argument. While courts may be an unnatural situs for correctional programs, very few transitions of probation from the judicial to the executive branch have required *local* probation departments attached to *local* government. Nearly all of the movement has been to a *statewide* agency located in the cabinet of the governor. Thus, the argument about courts is really an argument about state versus local control, which in turn devolves into a money-efficiency argument.

Before we go on to this economic issue, it is essential to reflect on the evolution of probation into a due process model. This evolution is not limited to probation alone; it has been common to corrections generally. If probation is an exercise of discretion and that discretion must be controlled by due process principles, then the court is the ultimate arbiter of what justice demands in the particular case. Since probation continues to be a court function, it seems anomalous, at best, to insist on a separation of probation from its natural setting in the courts. This, of course, is not to say that the arguments about the court's misuse of probation staff for its other needs or its weak administration are to be overlooked. These problems of management are real. They call for greater clarity of probation's goals and programs and independent administration. But in the long run the courts are a preferred setting for a due process model of corrections. One has only to think of the intrigue and delays which prisoners have experienced in getting their grievances before a judge to realize that probationers have distinct advantages of availability.

The central issue in the argument is a money-efficiency one. Money is a major and powerful argument, and rightly so. Whether it is the "preferred" sentencing alternative or not, probation is not used more by the courts because it does not have the resources to handle more people, especially criminal repeaters. Where probation services are sucked off into preparing presentence reports, there is little time for supervision or other community services that provide some assurance of protection for the community. The fact that probation is often touted as economical when compared with incarceration ignores the fact that probation figures frequently simply state the fact of undernourishment and underuse. If adequate services were provided, the gap between costs of incarceration and probation would be narrowed. In any event, nearly everyone argues that probation needs more money to do its job properly.

Following from this is the second leg of the argument. If more money is needed, only a state tax-base can supply it. Even if a few local governments can afford adequate probation services, not even they will be forthcoming for probation when so many other calls on the purse exist, especially when these are made more socially attractive. Further, many smaller jurisdictions simply do not have the dollars at all. Looking to the next level of government for public financing is typical, necessary, and inevitable. The state, it is said, can and should supply the money for adequate probation services statewide. One can easily see that it is a short and predictable jump to a *state-run system* of probation.

The answer to the money question is neither short nor easy. One might begin by suggesting that the medical model probation program, with its professional training and its one-to-one case approach, was more expensive than any jurisdiction could afford. On the other hand, the due process-reintegration model should be, in theory at least, much less expensive since the community is supplying the basic services. It is an important fact that the due process model provides a theoretical base for these services by arguing that the offender only loses those rights explicity taken away by law or necessarily implied in the sentence. Since the probationer is like other citizens except for these narrow disabilities, the community cannot discriminate against him in providing its services. The use of volunteers in the new approach to probation will also make adequate services less expensive.

Admitting all of this, one is still forced to accede to the point that probation is underfinanced. How can money be supplied short of "going state"? Creative solutions for this problem are not plentiful in the probation area because they have not been seen as critical. Only California and Washington have developed a state subvention plan whereby local probation is paid to reduce its commitments to state institutions. But surely other areas of state-local interest have explored this question of finance versus control and come up with something short of agglomerating local agencies into state government. If the value of retaining probation in the community were seen as important, solutions to the finance questions could be found.

This is the money side of the argument. The efficiency side is the heart of the matter and, although tied to budget, a separable issue. The Standards and Goals Commission's argument has the virtue of simplicity and forthrightness. It says that probation should join all other correctional programs at the state level in a single, comprehensive agency in order to unify the fragmented parts of the system. Obviously the matter cannot be that simple. Further explanations are in order. The Commission makes its argument hang on its central thesis of information and planning which, by a logic internal to the systems approach to structure, demands that fragmentation be replaced by unity, uniformity, and, ultimately, efficiency. Since the Commission makes no explicit argument for the unification of corrections, it does not give an adequate base for rebuttal except as one reads into the series of its reports the linkage among them with a concept of planning. Whatever the merits of an overall planning effort for all criminal justice agencies in a state, one can and must raise specific problems which complete administrative unification would bring. There seem to be three questions which the Commission chose to avoid answering in making its proposal for a unified state correctional agency.

First, there is no more devastating argument against true efficiency than creating an amalgam of traditionally diverse agencies which constitute a massive bureaucracy at the state level. In states like Illinois, New York, and California, personnel in these giant agencies would run into the tens of thousands. No more appalling situation can be imagined in which a single administrator would try to comprehend, conceptualize, and issue directives to these thousands. Surely the Commission is called upon to justify such an erratic recommendation beyond simple statements that a unified correctional agency would promote efficiency and uniformity.

Second, even if the Commission could come forward with management principles that would justify the creation of a monster agency, there are due process grounds on which it should be opposed. Reflecting on a similar study produced in New York six years ago (*Preliminary Report of the Governor's Special Committee on Criminal Offenders*, 1968), one is struck by the fact that this unified and comprehensive system would ensure that an offender would be the "client" (their term) of only one system. Whatever the sentencing alternative, there would be only a single place of commitment. The agency would become the only arbiter of how and when a criminal is treated. "Custody" would mean commitment and its meaning in each case would be determined by the officials of the agency. It does not take much imagination or paranoia to read into this plan a repressive type of regime controlled from a central headquarters. Even with the advent of the due process model to corrections, the problems would not be solved, only abated. The power of an agency that commanded massive budgetary resources would not easily accede to the orders of a single court. Once such an agency had made a judgment about an offender, he has no place to escape to, not even the courts. Fortunately, New York did not succumb to the charms of total efficiency, partly due, no doubt, to the resistance of existing agencies to the loss of identity in a monster mother-agency. One wonders if the traditional argument against a comprehensive state police agency is any less valid when it comes to unifying corrections. In terms of coercive intimacy, the exercise of the punitive jurisdiction is much more oppressive than that of law enforcement.

Third, the move to the state level carries with it a contradictory element vis-à-vis community-based corrections. If the role of the community in the new corrections is to be more window-dressing, as it should be, then putting probation within a large state agency is difficult to justify. How can it be an advantage to have probation administered at a statewide level as the central thrust of *community* corrections? The argument is made that a state agency is above the limitations of local politics. But this is hardly reassuring. Implied in this reference to local politics is a comparison to state politics, which, God knows, are not above pettiness or patronage. While local politics have hindered the development of a more professional staff for probation, this need not continue to be so. A state "merit" system can generate its own type of personnel problems that seem much less tractable than patronage problems. The argument is also made that a state agency will have access to greater resources which it can bring into the local community. The irony of that argument is that the services we are talking about are *social* services needed by everyone, not just offenders. If it would require the unification of corrections to bring needed social services to the local communities, then there is something vastly wrong with the system already.

Community-based corrections demands that the community have its role in the administration. It is difficult to imagine how a state-level agency would have any advantage—and not a great deal of disadvantage—in penetrating the community. Probation will still be initiated and controlled by the courts, which are local institutions. Offenders will be released to neighborhoods where the local community lives. Decisions about offenders will have immediate effect on these neighborhoods. Police will interact with offenders within local communities and policies will have to have careful local articulation. It seems difficult to accept a valid meaning for community in terms of a state agency administered from a central office and operating for efficiency and uniformity.

Conclusion

Whatever the direction of probation during the next decade, it seems implausible that the Commission's recommendations on a unified correctional agency will be acted on. On the other hand, the many solid suggestions and recommendations about the role of community in the new correctional model should get gradual acceptance and implementation. These fit in quite well with the due process model for corrections which the courts and offender litigants have fashioned over the past decade, as well as with the new philosophy of probation as reintegration.

NOTES

1. Mempa v. Rhay, 389 U.S. 128 (1967). Gagnon v. Scarpelli, 441 U.S. 778 (1973).
2. Mempa v. Rhay, 389 U.S. 128 (1967).
3. Gagnon v. Scarpelli, 411 U.S. 778 (1973).
4. People v. Hollis, 176 Cal. App. 2d 92 (1959); State v. Ivan, 33 N.J. 197 (1960).
5. State v. McCoy, 94 Idaho 236 (1971).
6. People v. Harpole, 97 Ill. App. 2d 28 (1968).
7. State v. Kunz, 55 N.J. 128 (1969); Ill. Rev. Stat., c. 38, §1005-3-4 (1973).

GILBERT GEIS

6. COMPENSATION TO VICTIMS OF VIOLENT CRIME

Victims of violent crime are among a wide array of losers in the lottery of contemporary existence. Indeed, it takes no great philosophical brooding to reach the conclusion that, in due time, each of us, in one way or another, will find ourselves on some casualty list. Kidneys give out, hearts fail, crippling lightning strikes, tornadoes descend, cars smash—indeed, the list of happenstance is limited only by the bounds of one's morbid imaginings.

Why,then, single out crime victims from the roster of social casualties for special reparative attention? Why employ state funds for their aid while other classes of victims, themselves also perfectly innocent, go unattended? The answer to this question pinpoints fundamental issues about social policy, legislative reality, and human nature. It responds to concerns about the form that compensation programs ought to take, if they are to take any form at all, and it speaks to challenges that an inroad in this area represents a significant concession by the state that will make it ultimately responsible for repairing the consequences of all unforeseen human deprivations.

Let it be noted, at the outset, that this question is a good deal more than a speculative academic exercise, divorced from practical realms. Ten American states now provide compensation to crime victims, using a variety of administrative arrangements, philosophical rationales, and eligibility structures. The United States Congress seems likely to enact legislation which would

Gilbert Geis is Professor in the Program in Social Ecology, University of California, Irvine, and author, with H. Edelhertz, of *Public Compensation to Victims of Crime* (1974).

allot substantial subsidies to states in the field, a move which would undoubtedly encourage those without programs to undertake them. In Canada, most of the provinces now have crime victim compensation programs, as do the majority of Australian states. The Canadian efforts differ particularly from most of the American systems by allowing eligibility to all crime victims, rather than only to those showing "serious financial hardship" (a term of art found in many of the American laws), and by tying their arrangements closely to those of workmen's compensation. The Australian schemes are rather placebolike enterprises which can be cited as indicative of state concern, while costing very little and helping very few.

New Zealand, which pioneered this area by inaugurating a victim compensation program in 1963, has now carried the matter to what might appear to be its logical conclusion by incorporating the crime victim compensation effort into a comprehensive no-fault insurance program, covering virtually all victims of debilitating events. Great Britain, which in 1964 followed New Zealand into the field, is in the process of providing a statutory foundation for its experimental *ex gratia* undertaking. The annual cost of the British program is now about $19 million dollars annually, a figure that needs to be regarded in terms of the widespread free medical services available in Britain and its relatively low crime rate compared to the United States.

In short, crime victim compensation programs are moving with inexorable progression into the governmental process. It is, of course, the nature of political life that social benefits, once granted, are very rarely retracted, as vested interest constituencies build up among actual and potential beneficiaries and within administrative bureaucracies. In this sense, perhaps, the issue of whether crime victims ought to be compensated is moot. They are being compensated, and they will increasingly be helped through the outlay of public funds. But these are still notably nascent programs, where they exist at all, and it appears worthwhile to look at their justifications and the forms that they have taken while there remains time and maneuvering space to shape them in a manner most suitable to their aims and ideologies. In addition, of course, information is now available from foreign and American programs to enable us to determine actual consequences more accurately. It would appear, therefore, that the prophesies on the likelihood of widespread fraud may not be quite accurate.

Opposition to Crime Victim Compensation

Crime victim compensation programs are notably attractive to politicians seeking platform issues likely to catch the attention of satiated and cynical mass media personnel. In New York, former Governor Rockefeller, for instance, cleverly intruded himself into a particularly brutal subway slaying of a man in front of his wife and infant by tying that episode into his advocacy of state victim compensation program. Few politicians overtly take issue with the idea of victim compensation; in the United States Senate, for instance, there are more than twenty co-sponsors with Senators McClellan and Mansfield of the current attempt to enact federal legislation. The federal attempt, though, has been unsuccessful for almost a decade, since Senator Ralph Yarborough first put a compensation bill before the Congress, an indication of what is probably legislative inertia as well as a current of covert opposition.

Opposition, when it does surface, is likely to take the form that crime victim compensation programs represent "creeping socialism," or, less polemically, that they constitute a drain on public funds urgently needed for more important government business. The latter view has been the basis for a continuing low-keyed holding operation against the federal measure on the part of the Nixon-Ford Administration, though the public explanation is apt to express a need for further study of the matter.

One of the sharpest statements of opposition to crime victim compensation appeared in a 1972 editorial in a Santa Ana, California, newspaper noted for its conservative convictions. The item, a comment on the proposed federal law, began with the observation that "the 'altruists' (with your money) are at it again," and went on to observe:

In other words, people who are unfortunate enough to become victims of illegal crime will be paid for any injury sustained, while you, minding your own business and innocent of any wrong doing, will be legally victimized in order to compensate those victimized illegally.

Put still another way, you are taxed once to pay for a system whose alleged function is to protect life, limb, and property, and then, when that system fails to do what it is paid to do, you are taxed again to pay for its failure.

Certainly, one of the more interesting between-the-lines elements of this editorial lies in its blithe assumption that the "you" it is addressing will inevitably be the one who pays for the victim compensation program rather than the one who collects from it. In this sense, it may be argued that at least some opposition stems not from the stated objection to double taxation— once for police support and once for victim compensation—but because the program is viewed primarily as a redistribution of wealth, with funds moving from the haves to the have-nots. Since crime victims do indeed come disproportionately from the lower socioeconomic strata, the grounds for the objection seem accurate enough. Whether they represent advocacy of a desirable social policy is, of course, a different matter.

More fundamentally, perhaps, the ethos underlying objections to crime victim compensation is one supporting a frontier spirit that presumably contributed to the vitality and independence that some commentators find notably attractive in American society. Risk-taking, calculated self-interest, personal saving for emergencies, and similar conditions, it is believed, would be undercut by systems in which unforeseen debilitating circumstances would be remedied by state resources derived from the more prudent or the more fortunate.

Opponents of crime victim compensation, in addition to ideological considerations, have also raised some practical objections. It has been stated, for instance, that such programs would encourage crime, first by providing offenders with a rationale for their behavior ("I am not seriously injuring anyone, since the state will reimburse him for his losses"), and second, by encouraging carelessness, since victims would know that expenses would not be permanent deprivations—presuming, at least, that crime-inflicted physical injuries would heal satisfactorily. There are further objections that the programs would encourage fraud, much as insurance schemes in the automobile field seem rife with fictitious and inflated claims. Indeed, it is sometimes maintained that part of the cynicism of the professional thief comes from his bemusement at lists of items that he allegedly had stolen, when these appear in newspapers before being submitted to insurance adjustors.

Disputations regarding the impact of crime victim compensation on the quality of the American way of life, while fundamental to the question of whether such compensation ought to be allowed, are not resolvable by empirical data. Antagonists to crime victim compensation programs on ideological grounds traditionally state as unassailable positions which are, at best, arguable. The moral decline and depravity of the country, they may insist, is clearly traceable to government blundering and interference in its economic and social life. Their opponents insist that laissez faire is a shield and rallying slogan for the vicious exercise by the entrenched of unbridled self-interest, and that it is contrary to the compassion expected in a country with a strong religious heritage. They argue that crime victim compensation programs bring American society closer to the essence of a democratic form of government, one in which minority positions are protected, the needy are aided, and each person is enabled to achieve the best he can as long as he does not undermine a similar pursuit by others.

Persons operating from the latter framework note that public funds currently are available for a wide range of private matters, and that philosophical debate concentrating on the extension of an idea already deeply embedded in political life is anachronistic. The proper question, they say, is not whether government money ought to be employed to help people in need, but only whether crime victims represent a class of citizens who should be aided now. And, if the judgment is affirmative, they maintain, the next step is to examine the grounds upon which such a decision can be translated into action.

Advocacy of Victim Compensation

The simplest line of reasoning offered by proponents of crime victim compensation programs is that such efforts appear "reasonable" as responses to citizen concern about crime in the streets, and that they represent an idea, to use the cliché often employed in such matters, "whose time has come." A representation in this vein has been put forward by an English legal scholar, Rupert Cross:

> I am content to do without theoretical justifications. . . . After all, these are questions of public welfare and they should be determined by public opinion. Human needs account for the most of the Welfare State, and its evolution has nothing to do with tortuous reasoning. . . . If there is a widely recognized hardship, and if that hardship can be cheaply remedied by state compensation, I should have thought that the case for such a remedy was made out, provided the practical difficulties are not too great. The hardship in these cases is undoubtedly widely recognized.[1]

If the premises of Cross's position are admitted, it becomes necessary to determine the existence of some of the conditions he posits as necessary for the inauguration of compensation programs. This can be done initially by examining the manner in which crime victims are treated by the criminal justice system, and by looking at their deprivation as a consequence of crime victimization. Efforts can also be made to determine the state of public opinion on the issue of crime victim compensation, and to figure out methods and costs of remediation.

Plight of the Crime Victim

With the exception of the police, no segment of the criminal justice system is spared the victim's deep anger and intense disdain. The police are generally regarded favorably by victims of crimes of violence, and particularly by women (with the notable exception of rape victims) and less positively by victims of property crimes. In general, crime victims believe that their needs have low priority in the courts and the correctional system. They feel that they are, at best, tolerated, and then often with grace-less ill-humor. Their role, they say, seems much like that of the expectant father in the hospital at delivery time: necessary for things to have gotten underway in the past, but at the moment rather superfluous and mildly bothersome. Crime victims will sometimes note that the offender seems to fare a good deal better than they do; he is regarded by criminal justice function-aries as a doer, an antagonist, someone to be wary of, a person who must be manipulated successfully if the workers in the criminal justice system are to have satisfaction and rewards for a job well done.

The victim, on the other hand, is part of the background scenery—a rather drab character, in the nature of a spear-carrying supernumerary, watching from a distance the preening and posturing of the prima donna stars in the criminal justice drama. There have been occasional frank acknowledgments of this condition. "Railroads for some time have not done much to please the customer," attorney David Epstein has noted. "Our system has been behaving like a railroad, because maybe it figures the crime victim can't just choose another court system. We've got to look at the victim like he's a customer who requires service."

Richard Kuh, New York City's district attorney, tells from the inside some of the buffetings visited upon the victim of crime as he seeks "justice":

I have seen complainants scolded and harassed by judges, and I will say by prosecutors, including myself, and when they have said to us, "I will not come down again. I have been here twelve times and every time I am here, there is some reason for adjourn-ment, and I cannot miss any more days at work. I just will not come again."

And I as a prosecutor have had—and I might say it is the most hateful thing I have done in my years of prosecution—I have had the problem of telling these complainants we have no alternative but to hold you in contempt if you don't come again.

Even these kinds of expressions of concern with the situation of the crime victim are rare, so insignificant do victims appear to those engaged in the process of handling criminal offenses. In this regard, the President's Commission on Law Enforcement and Administration of Justice noted that "one of the most neglected subjects in the study of crime is its victims, the persons, households and businesses that bear the brunt of crime in the United States." A law professor echoes this observation: "Surely there will be agreement," Professor Childres has written, "that some attention should be diverted from the criminal, one of the most rigorously studied animals in history, to his victim, one of the most ignored."

Victim compensation awards would not, of course, be totally responsive to the kinds of malaise indicated in the foregoing materials. They could, however, serve some palliative purpose, allowing the victim to gain a feeling that his plight is understood and that he is being afforded tangible evidence of sympathy. In addition to this, there is a strong need for the criminal justice system to learn some rudimentary manners, if nothing else. Common courtesy would dictate that, among other things, crime victims ought to be thanked for their efforts, both in person and by letter, and ought to be told about the disposition of their case and the reasons for the outcome.

Consequences of Victimization. There are both concrete and more subtle kinds of losses from victimization by crimes against the person. In regard to the former, a good deal of case history material exists in reports from crime victim compensation programs now in operation. In New York, for instance, until fiscal considerations stemming from a burgeoning caseload dictated curtailment in 1970, each application received by the Criminal Injuries Compensation Board during the year was summarized in its annual report. Page after page of this material indicates the often-tragic and, except for the existence of the compensation program, otherwise irreparable consequences of victimization in regard to medical expenses and loss of earnings.

Beyond such materials, there is little information on the costs to victims of violent crime. Two rather cursory Canadian studies—one carried out in British Columbia and the second in Ontario—indicate that about 60 percent of the crime victims surveyed there had incurred medical expenses (the average unreimbursed total was about $40.00), and 40 percent had suffered some loss of income (averaging about $100.00). Not surprisingly, more than 80 percent of the victimized persons believed that there should be a compensation program for crime victims.

A more detailed study was conducted by Sylvia Fogelman of 170 persons in Los Angeles County who had applied for victim compensation during the period between November 1, 1969, and October 31, 1970. Of the forty-nine persons who completed the questionnaire (a 29-percent response), ten had been granted compensation, twenty had been denied it, and nineteen had cases that were still pending. The average age of the respondents was forty-two years. In about 75 percent of the cases, the applicants themselves were the crime victims.

More than half of the cases involved assault with a deadly weapon, and half of these had an element of robbery in them. A typical situation, as described by the victim, was: "I was shot after I could not fulfill the robber's request for money." In a large majority of cases (86 percent), the perpetrator of the crime was a stranger to the victim.

Some of the respondents may have exaggerated their injuries because their claims were still pending. But it remains noteworthy that more than 60 percent stated that their injury left permanent damage. Forty percent maintained that they were functioning at a lower level of employment following the criminal incident than prior to it, and many indicated that they could no longer hold a job. Typical comments were: (1) ". . . still disabled . . . medical examination has ruled out my being able to take up training for my sort of work for the time being;" (2) ". . . because of permanent injuries, I have been medically dismissed from my job;" (3) ". . . trying to attend Adult Community School to brush up on shorthand, typing, and prep for civil service exam; . . . Aerospace was my background and last job (11 years) but impossible to return to my old company—no jobs . . . and, of course, I am unable to cope with an 8 to 5 job at present." Among those who stated that the injury had no effect on their employment, 22 percent were nonemployed individuals, such as housewives, students, and retired persons.

102

Two-thirds of the respondents indicated that the crime against them had affected their social life, primarily in regard to loss of friends and lessened ability to function socially. More than 70 percent said that they had felt an immediate need to talk to someone to sort out their problems and get back on their feet. Yet more than a quarter of this group had not found anyone to discuss these matters with, and the comment "no one seems to care" was common in their responses. Even with an average expiration of fourteen months since the crimes, 40 percent of the respondents still expressed a need for counseling. These were primarily women; more than twice as many women as men expressed such a need.

It must be appreciated that crime victims only rarely are able to see themselves as entirely guiltless persons who have no necessity to review their action and attitudes in order to understand what had happened to them. If nothing else, they must satisfactorily resolve questions relating to the lottery of human existence which resulted in injury being visited upon them rather than upon another. They must also have some anodynic answer to the question "Why me?" or thereafter must become confirmed in the discomforting position that existence is hopelessly haphazard, and that there is no gain to be had from rational, self-protective, planned action.

Too many alternative ways of behaving usually had been available to the crime victim (unlike, say, the cancer victim) to allow much ready surcease from soul-searching; a better door lock, more care in choosing the route to one's destination, availability of a gun or other weapon, more awareness of the danger from certain kinds of persons—these and a host of other "but if's" nag at the crime victim. Presumably, some reinforcement for the view that they are, indeed, innocent and deserving victims of misfortune could be had by those suffering the consequences of crimes against the person if the state were to accord them reparations.

Public Opinion. The will of the majority of the population may not be the most compelling rationale for public policy; after all, the majority may well be favorable to things violative of basic principles of justice and decency. But in regard to matters such as crime victim compensation, the opinions of citizens would seem to be a fairly reasonable gauge of whether a society is "ready for" such a program.

A nationwide poll on the subject was conducted in 1965 by the Gallup people. It found that 62 percent of the adult population answered affirmatively to the question: "Suppose an innocent person is killed by a criminal—do you think the state should make financial provisions for the victim's family?" This is, of course, the extreme situation in victim compensation, much of which is concerned with assaults and similar kinds of nonlethal incidents. On the other hand, the example could have been made a good deal more dramatic, in terms of an itemization of the fiscal and psychological trauma and needs of the survivors.

At any rate, only 29 percent of the respondents did not believe the survivors should be compensated, and 9 percent offered no opinion. No differences were found between men and women on the issue, though there was a tendency for persons with lesser amounts of education and jobs in agriculture or those involving manual labor to be more favorable to compensation than persons in business and the professions. There was no significant difference among persons identifying themselves as Republicans, Democrats, or "Independent" voters, though support for reparation was somewhat higher in the South (67 percent affirmative) and the East (65 percent) than in the West (59 percent) and the Midwest (56 percent). As might have been anticipated, the higher a person's income the less likely he was to favor state compensation for the family of the victimized person. More surprising was the variation in community size and response, with residents of rural areas registering greater approval of the idea of compensation (66 percent) than residents of the largest metropolitan cities, those with populations of more than a half a million persons (59 percent).

The Gallup survey can be supplemented by the results of a poll conducted late in 1967 among professionals working in the criminal justice field in regard to their views about victim compensation. The work was done by J. Walter Thompson, an advertising agency, at the request of the *Reader's Digest,* which was interested in generating promotional material to supplement an article that had been carried in its July 1967 issue, "The *Victims* of Crime Deserve a Break." Some 7,652 questionnaires were dispatched to persons on a mailing list supplied by the National Council on Crime and Delinquency (NCCD), and 1,719 responses were received (22.5 percent). The results have not previously been published.

Most notable from the questionnaires is the overwhelming support for victim compensation among these professionals, though it should be kept in mind that the NCCD list undoubtedly was biased in the direction of having more "concerned" persons on it. An initial survey question read: "Do you feel that the state should compensate victims of criminal acts?" Just short of 90 percent of the respondents thought that it should. Table 1 indicates the differentiation of answers by the occupations of the respondent; an interesting ingredient is the fact that, though all groups are heavily favorable to the idea, judges are considerably less enthusiastic than the remaining groups.

Other questionnaire responses showed an almost even division in regard to support of "federal legislation to assure uniform treatment of victims in different states"—48.6 percent favored the idea, 48.5 opposed it, and 2.9 percent did not supply an answer. Eighty percent of the sample agreed that administration of

TABLE 1

Endorsement of the Idea of State Compensation to Crime Victims (by professional background)

Background	Number	Percent Favorable	Percent Unfavorable	Percent No Answer
Police Officials	26	92.3	7.7	0
Correction Officials	951	89.0	9.7	1.3
Judges	101	84.2	12.9	2.9
Youth and Other Agency Officials	355	92.1	6.5	1.4
Academics	255	91.1	6.2	2.7
Miscellaneous	61	91.8	6.6	1.6
TOTALS	1,719	89.8	8.6	1.6

victim compensation programs under welfare department auspices, as California had attempted, "weakens" the thrust of victim compensation, while 73 percent favored a separate administrative agency to oversee compensation such, as the one that exists in New York.

Public opinion, then, both among the general citizenry and among a sample of professionals closely acquainted with the criminal justice system, demonstrates a high level of support for establishment of crime victim compensation. The need can be seen to exist, therefore, and the state of public opinion is favorable. The final issue is one of feasibility: are such programs possible to mount, how might they best be structured, and what will they cost?

Operational Issues

The existence of ten American state programs for crime victim compensation indicates beyond peradventure that they can be viable government efforts. Some of these programs, indeed, are beginning to approach their first decade of work. Nonetheless, it is notable that quite diverse paths have been taken in the programs, and that considerable debate continues regarding the "model" method, if such a method exists, for handling crime victim compensation problems.

Questions that must be addressed include, among others, the matter of eligibility for compensation in terms of the events to be covered by the program. Eligibility may be established in regard to specified violent crimes or in light of the consequences of an offense. Arson, for example, is generally not regarded as a crime against the person, but often produces severe personal injury; should it be a compensable offense? There are also problems concerned with the manner in which possible involvement of victims in the perpetration of an offense should bear on their right to be compensated. Such involvement could disqualify them for assistance, or it could be used to reduce the amount to which they are entitled. A third view, expressed by Baroness Wootton during parliamentary debates on the British compensation scheme, is that such issues ought not be relevant:

I think the end of this story will be that it will be found impossible to determine the measure of fault of the victim . . . This attempt to assess people's needs after they have suffered serious and possibly permanent injury by the question of whether it is their fault or anybody else's fault is an illogical and uncivilized approach to the subject.

Other questions that must be dealt with in programs to compensate crime victims include the following: Should crimes involving members of the same family entitle the injured person to receive aid? Sixty-five percent of the *Reader's Digest* survey respondents thought not. How should such relationships be defined, particularly in this day of rather amorphous kinds of living arrangements? Should payments be granted in a lump sum, or should they be awarded over a period of time with provisions for regular review? Should there be minimums and maximums on awards? Should individuals who possess adequate financial resources nonetheless be given compensation? Should appeals from decisions regarding compensation be allowed, or should an administrative finding represent the final determination of the matter?

Answers to questions such as these are basically related to conceptions of the reasons why the state should undertake to compensate victims of violent crime and the purposes such compensation seeks to achieve. If, for instance, the goal of assistance is to return all persons who have been thrust out of the social stream because of violent crime as near as possible to "normal" living, it seems reasonable that contributory negligence on their part, at least to the extent that it is short of behavior that violates the law, should not interfere with the amount of the award. If program justification lies in the view that the state owes an obligation to its citizens for not protecting them adequately, the failure of a victim to have taken reasonable advantages of resources afforded by the state should disqualify him or her from compensation. Negligence in heeding police warnings about traversing certain city areas after dark, failure to cooperate with a police investigation, and similar behavior, given such a rationale for compensation, would disqualify a victim from state aid.

Plans for compensation of victims also must be evaluated in terms of their impact upon various social arrangements. The relationship between compensation and crime rates, if any, needs to be studied. The impact of victim compensation on the rehabilitation of offenders also represents a question about which only speculative answers are presently possible. Interestingly, a program is now underway in Minnesota in which prison inmates voluntarily come together with the victims of their offenses and establish a mutually acceptable contract setting the terms by which the offender will satisfy his "obligation" to the victim. This approach—at the moment restricted to property offenders —indicates the kinds of arrangements that might emerge as state-funded victim compensation systems undergo careful scrutiny.

Components of Programs

A review of some major characteristics of existing crime victim compensation programs in the United States provides an indication of differing resolutions of basic questions relating to the delivery of reparation services. We will concentrate, in particular, on descriptions of the two oldest American programs, the one in California, and the other in New York. This review can be supplemented by the reader through examination of model statutes which provide the results of the thinking of panels of specialists trying to put together what they regard as "ideal" program outlines—outlines which are not as constrained by the political exigencies that usually mark bargaining in the legislative arena.

California. On July 1, 1974, the California program began to operate under amended legislation which sought to update, expand, and clarify the 1965 state statute which was the pioneering effort in crime victim compensation in the United States. The new law raised the maximum allowable award from the previous $5,000, an amount which had been the most niggardly in the United States, to $23,000, with that figure involving a $10,000 ceiling on medical and/or burial expenses, $10,000 on losses of wages or support, and $3,000 for vocational rehabilitation. The provision of job training for crime victims does not appear anywhere else in the American array of compensation programs. The California law requires a showing of "serious financial hardship" for eligibility, though this condition may be established prospectively, that is, if the crime victim is able to demonstrate that victimization costs will deplete his current and expected resources. Only three states, it might be noted—Hawaii, Massachusetts, and Washington—do not require a showing of financial need in order to qualify for victim compensation.

California added a unique clause in 1974 which allows compensation for injuries or death sustained by the victim of a driver who commits a hit-and-run offense, or is involved in drunk driving, or driving under the influence of narcotics. Attorneys fees are set at a ceiling of $500. (California state officials, though, have been surprised at the relatively low level of client representation, since the work involved, they believe, is more than adequately compensated by allowable legal fees.) The minimum recoverable amount for the victim is established at whichever is lower: (1) $100.00; or (2) 20 percent or more of the victim's net monthly income. California now has inserted some teeth into its requirement that law enforcement officers must notify victims of the existence of the compensation programs by providing that the Attorney General may require police organizations to file descriptions of the procedures they have adopted to achieve this end.

Other provisions in the new California law resemble those generally found in most American jurisdictions. Failure to cooperate with law enforcement officers, for instance, is grounds for disqualification. Negligence or provocation are also matters which can void an application or reduce an award. The state can attempt through subrogation processes to recover its expenditures from the offender. Also, the offender need not be apprehended, found guilty, or be capable of being found guilty (as in instances of nonage or insanity) for the victim to be eligible for assistance.

In California, unlike most states, the compensation program is administered by a preexisting agency, the Board of Control, which, among other things, also handles tort claims against the state, as well as the Good Samaritan program. Before 1967, the

California victim compensation program had been operated by the Department of Social Welfare, in what was a disastrous episode, largely because of the Department's inability to treat crime victims as other than charity cases, deserving of nothing better than the harassment and condescension often accorded to welfare clients.

New York. The New York victim compensation program is the largest in the nation. In 1972 to 1973, for instance, it made approximately 900 awards on the basis of about 2,500 claims. The cost of awards was more than 1.7 million dollars and administrative expenses ran to more than $400,000. Impetus for inauguration of the program followed the fatal stabbing of a twenty-eight-year-old man in a New York City subway in late 1965. The ensuant legislation established a three-member (it has since expanded to five persons) Crime Victims Compensation Board, and marked the first use of "serious financial hardship" as an eligibility requirement. The genesis of this provision has been explained by the New York Board Chairman:

. . . our legislature had already been badly bitten by Medicaid. They were told one thing and when it got into existence, it blossomed. They treated this victim compensation program as another one of those runaways, and that's why they actually put serious financial hardship in it.[2]

The Board itself has come to regard the hardship requirement as unjustifiable and irksome, particularly because it forecloses awards to victims who have been frugal and accumulated personal resources, while it allows those who were more profligate with similar incomes to collect aid from the state. In addition, the Board has come to believe that broadening eligibility to all crime victims would be relatively inexpensive, perhaps adding 10 to 20 percent to the annual budget, and would provide easier administration (background investigations would not have to be so thorough) and better public relations.

New York recently changed to an approach under which the claimant bears the burden of supplying materials to establish his compensability, a procedure that sometimes antagonizes applicants, who complain of bureaucracy or invasion of privacy in regard to calls for copies of income tax returns. Payments are now made by the Board to creditors instead of directly to applicants when there are outstanding bills. A serious lag in the time between original application and awards has also begun to intrude into the New York program. The Board is at present seriously weighing putting a limit on medical expenses, largely because of their escalation during the past few years. The New York program has a general maximum, from which medical expenses are excepted, of $15,000. As the first persons to have received that total are using up their award, Board members are beginning to become concerned about the fundamental aims of their program and the relationship of the statutory provisions to such aims. The Board maintains that close investigations have uncovered very few instances of fraud, though it grants that there has been some tendency to camouflage resources. Claims are generally handled by a single Board member, with appeals going to the entire Board.

Other Programs. Highlights from the remaining eight crime victim compensation programs offer a sampling of ingredients of the operations that have been mounted in the different jurisdictions. Hawaii in many ways has the most interesting of the programs.[3] It is the only state, for instance, which permits "pain and suffering" awards. And, from 1968 until 1972, Hawaii allowed collateral recovery from victim compensation when a victim also had been paid by private insurance or by workman's compensation; in 1972, however, the legislature decided that this was too liberal an approach. The Hawaii program is run much in the manner of a state tort claims system. A part-time Commissioner makes awards, after which the legislature appropriates funds to cover the amounts granted.

The Hawaii statute had indicated that the Criminal Injuries Compensation Commission could "consider any circumstances it determines to be relevant" in making awards, and it was supposed that this mandate would be translated into a "needs" provision. Commission members, however, faced with actual claimants, decided otherwise. It might be noted that in 1972, Hawaii, with one twenty-third the population of New York, provided crime victims with about one-tenth as much as was given in

New York. In terms of people served, New York made awards to only four times as many individuals as did Hawaii. If the same rate and ratio of payment were made in New York as in Hawaii (where one out of eight reported victims received aid), the New York program cost would rise from near $2 million to about 35 million dollars with another 14 million dollars (39 percent) necessary if New York included pain and suffering awards equivalent to those granted in Hawaii.

The Massachusetts program is markedly different from the others in the United States in its use of the courts as the adjudicating agency for victimization claims. In general, it appears that this mechanism has served to keep claimants from seeking aid to the extent that they do elsewhere, partly because of the awkwardness of arrangements and partly because the courts are by law warned to "take into consideration . . . the availability of funds appropriated . . . " before granting assistance. In this regard, awards often remain unpaid for long periods of time. Location of the program was placed under court auspices after a study commission concluded that compensation decisions are judicial in nature, and that "neighborhood" courts would be in a better position to determine the nature of the claimants' situation. It was also believed that the extra work burden could reasonably be borne by existing personnel and facilities. Judges, though, may not sit on a compensation claim and a criminal prosecution growing out of the same occurrence, since this would be prejudicial to the criminal defendant's rights. Absence of a central authority responsible for the Massachusetts program is regarded as one of its major weaknesses.

The Maryland program is noted for its high ceiling, ($45,000), a function of the attachment of the program to the fiscal arrangements of workmen's compensation. Particularly noteworthy in the Maryland law is a provision that has judges impose an additional $5 fine in all cases except motor vehicle violations to help fund the program. In the past three years, these fines have averaged $150,000 annually, covering about 7 percent of the cost of the crime victim compensation effort. The Maryland law also includes the unusual provision that a fine of not less than $500.00 or one-year imprisonment can be imposed on persons filing fraudulent claims. In this regard, perhaps because of its proximity to major population centers in adjoining jurisdictions, Maryland seems to be particularly beset by claims based on acts occurring elsewhere. "We have had a considerable amount of problems with crimes that occur close to the D.C. line. They crawl over the line," the Maryland chairman noted at an administrators' conference.[4]

The remaining five programs—those of New Jersey, Alaska, Washington, Louisiana, and Illinois—have been operating for only a short period of time. The New Jersey effort, except for the absence of a need provision, is much like the program of New York, and is run by a three-member Violent Crimes Compensation Board. In Alaska, the compensation program is operated by an administrative agency which delegates hearing functions to other officials, who must be attorneys. Board members themselves need not have legal backgrounds, but one member is required to be a medical or osteopathic physician, a stipulation not found elsewhere. The Louisiana legislation located the administrative function for crime victim compensation in the Board of Review of the Department of Employment Security. The statute includes a financial need showing before reimbursement, and lists a roster of crimes for which victim compensation might be available. The Washington statute, effective in mid-year 1974, places the victim compensation program within the Department of Labor and Industries. The Washington measure has the most detailed provision in the United States regarding recovery from the offender of moneys expended under the act. Benefits to or on behalf of the victim create "a debt due and owing to the department by any person found to have committed such criminal act in either a civil or criminal court proceeding in which he is a party." The amount may be recovered from work release wages or its payment set as a condition of parole, though the amount due also may be waived, modified downward, or otherwise adjusted by the department in the interest of justice and the rehabilitation of the individual. In Illinois, the statute, enacted in 1973, sets a minimum of $500.00 on compensation awards, and has applications processed by the Court of Claims. Whether this recourse to judicial tribunals, following the path of Massachusetts, proves more successful in Illinois, is one of the more interesting issues relating to delivery of compensation to crime victims that awaits resolution.

Conclusion

Fundamentally, programs designed to compensate persons injured by crimes of violence are attempts to placate a public opinion often unnerved and resentful of what is viewed as a rising tide of aggressive criminal activity. In this respect, the present emergence of such schemes can most readily be understood as a response to ever-increasing degrees of anonymity, urban living, juvenile precocity, social change, and other crime-related factors in the United States and throughout the world.

A certain spirit of communal responsibility is also gradually pervading the contemporary world. This attitude may also lie behind the payment of public money to individuals who have been deprived of their livelihood, have been subjected to unusual expenses for personal injury, or have lost their source of support because of violent crime. This spirit is by no means altogether new; what is noteworthy are the expanding realms it has come to embrace.

Of the two major components of the spirit underlying victim compensation, then, one is essentially compassionate: People have been hurt through no fault of their own; it is a moral obligation of those more fortunate to assist them. The second element arises from an economic rationality which suggests that failure to make adequate provisions for incapacitated persons ultimately deprives all members of the society of common benefits.

Public programs and debates regarding crime victim compensation tend to revolve around such matters as administrative arrangements, costs, and eligibility requirements. These items have a way of turning attention away from the personal factors which gave rise to the whole matter, the plight of crime victims. In part, the victims' stories are repetitious, and almost any kind of suffering, however intense, tends to become dulled in its impact if repeated too often. In part, too, there is a reluctance to move too close to the victim, out of a sensitivity urging that invasion of a sufferer's privacy is graceless and voyeuristic. Repeated stories of awful misery among crime victims also can create as much discomfort and frustration among nonvictims as they can arouse empathy.

Nonetheless, in any discussion of compensation programs, a vision of the situation of the crime victim must firmly be kept in mind. Sometimes, of course, victims have precipitated their own doom; often their lives are less than tidy and innocent. Often, though, they are guilty of nothing more than bad luck, being in the wrong place at the wrong time. In either event, they are human beings with serious problems, needing help. Conversations with administrators of compensation programs often turn to specific cases they encountered, instances in which they were moved to deep compassion or were intensely saddened. This, it must be remembered, is what crime victim compensation basically is all about.

NOTES

1. Rupert Cross, "Compensating Victims of Violence," *The Listener* 49 (May 16, 1963), p. 816.
2. Stanley L. Van Renssalaer, at Second International Conference on Compensation of Innocent Victims of Violent Crime, *Proceedings,* Baltimore, May 27–29, 1970, p. 33
3. Hawaii Rev. Stat. §351-1 (1968).
4. Third International Conference on the Compensation of Victims of Crime: Toronto, 1972, p. 87.

III

CORRECTIONAL REFORM

DAVID FOGEL

7. PRISON: THE FORTRESS MODEL vs. THE JUSTICE MODEL

Anyone with more than a passing knowledge of criminal justice knows that a system for its administration hardly exists. One speaks of the subsystems (police, prosecution, courts and corrections) as discrete entities relating to each other in response to offender transactions. One must move with caution since it is not at all clear that the subparts represent subsystems rather than simply a convenient rubric for categorizing similar functions.

Since the present analysis concerns itself with corrections, let us inquire briefly into it as a "system." An operational definition is first in order. Corrections represents the experience of an offender or alleged offender after arrest: during initial jail incarceration in a pretrial state, in any of a number of growing pretrial diversion programs, in posttrial care for those ajudged guilty, in jails and prisons, in nonincarcerative programs, and the pre- and postprison experiences called probation and parole. These experiences are supervised by private organizations, by chiefs of police, sheriffs, district attorneys, judges, city and state commissioners of corrections, or attorneys general. The keeper and the kept are spread out on a jurisdictional continuum from federal to village. The accident of geography will determine any of the present 430,000 prisoners' supervision and opportunity structure on a given day.

David Fogel is Executive Director of the Illinois Law Enforcement Commission and former Commissioner of the Minnesota Department of Corrections.

For example, there exist a federal system of prisons, and a federal probation and parole system, a contractual system for post prison care with the private sector, and public pretrial detention facilities. The federal system also has a reciprocal contractual relationship with some of the states for the care of state prisoners and in turn the states care for some federal prisoners. We now find fifty state prison systems and a major-city system (New York City's rivals New York State's in size) and some 3,000 county jail systems. Only a handful of states have unified, statewide systems for prisons and jails. Probation and sometimes even parole find themselves being hosted by a county judge, by a circuitwide administrator, by a state corrections commission, or as an entirely separate agency of local or state government. Sometimes the state contracts to operate probation services for a court. Sometimes probation and parole caseloads are merged locally; and either the state contracts to have its parolees supervised by the local court or probation officer, or the latter contracts with the state to have its probation case load supervised by the state parole officer located in the area. Much depends upon whether the local community has an independent probation department or whether the latter simply operates at and for the convenience of the court. Statewide uniform probation systems, independent of the courts, are few.

An integrated criminal justice system does not exist and even its subsystems are simply fragmented subparts—themselves not integrated entities. An examination of the other subparts— police, courts, and prosecution—would show similar fragmentation. One may imagine the prisoner arriving at a state prison after bewildering encounters with the agencies of justice along a very bumpy continuum.

If the first fact of prison life is the randomness of the system, then the second could reasonably be its anachronistic physical setting. The architecture of the fortress prison and its geographical setting are enough themselves to defeat any rehabilitative purpose it may claim. Set in the most part in remote rural areas, built in the style of the last century, the fortress prison is layer upon layer of steel cages set in concrete behind massive walls.

The Fortress Prison

Over the last two centuries we have developed around the fortress prison an arsenal of religio-clinical appendages. Men and women from several professional disciplines have been able to enter the correctional arena, present a panacea and capture the attention of the keeper and the kept for a time. The literature is embarrassingly replete with simplistic solutions. They represent a curious admixture of religious, moral, and psychological fervor sometimes coupled with unbridled barbarism. The introduction of the case method of psychological treatment and all its variants has always had the shadow of punishment cast over its efforts. The fortress prison in one form or another survives, sometimes with a hospital look like Maryland's Patuxent and sometimes with the quality of instant obsolesence like Ohio's pastel Lucasville.

The several disciplines have used these institutions as professional playgrounds with little demonstrable gain in public safety. A voluminous literature has developed. An unprecedented polarity has occurred between the professional and the guard and between the latter and the inmate. An economic chasm has been opened between the guard and all other actors in criminal justice. Left in the fortress prison are the angry and inappropriate antagonists—keeper and kept—playing out a drama of escalating confrontation which promises to reach epic proportion.

With some few but notable exceptions, adult corrections can in composite be reasonably described as a 150-year-old warehouse. It imprisons an increasing number of the poor, more outspoken, urban minorities and is staffed by poorly paid, low status, second-, sometimes third-generation custody officers. The medium is the message. Steel and concrete do not mix with humanity and rehabilitation. Adding caseworkers or psychiatrists to this milieu has not produced basic change. Nor is it fruitful to conceptualize, as some prison officials are wont to do, the current rash of prison riots as conspiracies perpetrated by political militants—usually Black. Each disturbance usually reveals a range of contributing circumstances, from neglect of massive problems to aimless escalations of minor events. The presumption underlying the conspiratorial notion of our current strife is that the prison and its administrators always remain faultless in what should, in their rationale, otherwise remain a stable institution. Human dignity is reaching a new plateau which some administrators have fearfully mistaken for a widespread conspiracy among a "new breed" of inmates. Prison history is full of such excuses and alibis. If legislatures are not providing enough resources, it is because they are probably tired of escalating costs and declining results after more than 150 years of support. Without public involvement and legislative support, prisons remain expensive, latent volcanoes of violence with reforms destined never to outlive reformers.

The third fact of prison life is the correctional officer, a central actor in this drama. He can be brushed off as a brutal Neanderthal type or he can be enlisted as an agent of change and find a new dignity for himself. We can no longer afford the futility of polarization. The massive social problems of America are felt inside our prisons as well as outside. We just play them out with more savagery inside. A police chief in Maryland once told me after his first extended visit to a prison that he had been inside a cancer, and that if we did not arrest its growth, it would envelop free society too.

The correctional officer had an easier job in the early days. All he needed was a club, a steel-tipped cane, and a rifle or a whip to administer a silent lock-step system of prison behavior management. His mission was simply, "hold on to these convicts."

Put yourselves into the shoes of a correctional officer for a two-minute historical trip. You would have seen a series of new professionals entering the system, ostensibly to help you: ministers, academic educators, production foreman, vocational educators, recreation supervisors. You noted that all this specialized help created an adverse effect on your mission—security and custody. They never worked nights or weekends or got much involved when sporadic violence broke out. In addition to all the new problems they brought with them, these folks were now making considerably more money than you.

That was the first wave. Then your bosses discovered a number of other helping professions and introduced social workers, psychologists, psychiatrists, occupational, speech and even music therapists.

These folks, too, for the most part, worked Monday to Friday, 9 to 5. They also made more money and they made even more compromises with the basic mission—custody. To make you feel better, you were now told that you were part of a "treatment or rehabilitation team." Whenever a new fad broke out it swept through the system. One state prided itself on the fact that it had divided its inmate population into hundreds of therapy groups and that hundreds of its correctional officers were now "group therapists." Responding to this process of innovation through rhetoric, many convicts called it the biggest collective farce of the century.

As a member of a treatment team you learned that convicts have emotional needs, psyches, ethnic pride, and are due respect. Finally, you witnessed a medical revolution which introduced a hundred new pills into the prison—to be dispensed for the most part by you. You wondered just what they expected of you. These changes over time gave you less status in the prison and a contradictory, fragmented job to do—not exactly a bonus from history.

While we have made some progress in the behavioral sciences and introduced new, promising programs into corrections, the correctional officer has remained the unaffected, even disaffected, professional fossil. Very little has touched him but the rhetoric of reform and treatment. He is rightly discouraged and angry. At the National Prison Congress meeting of 1970, the Secretary of the California Prison Commission pointed out that the training of the correctional officer is the reform which needs to precede all other prison reforms for it contains in it the seed of all else as surely as the acorn contains the oak.

Of those who work in a prison the correctional officer has the toughest hours, the most hazardous work style, is closest to the convict, has the least status, prestige, and recognition from both his colleagues and the public. Compound these indignities further by his being the lowest paid among correctional jobs and least educated, and a detailed image begins to emerge.

These officers are mainly rural, often second and sometimes third generation. They are called upon to supervise angry young men who are increasingly from urban areas and minority groups.

Cultural barriers are frequently compounded by language barriers.

The prison and its personnel have historically experienced isolation from the public and other public and private agencies. Until the late 1960s prisoners' access to the courts was quite limited since the prevailing view by the latter of the former was that of "slave of the state" with virtually no recognizable rights beyond life itself. The courts quite plausibly maintained a "hands off" doctrine in relation to prisoners' petitions.

Into this milieu, over the years, have been introduced dozens of theories of criminality and treatment regimens to accompany them. None of them worked effectively. The public, police agencies, academia, legislators, the press, and indeed the prisoner-as-consumer of the correctional service all substantially agree that the prison degrades, is unsafe, does not correct, and does little to enhance the public safety.

The prison, then, has developed mindlessly over the last two centuries as a part of a nonsystem of criminal justice. It is located in physically remote sites and employs various unsuccessful regimens. Its personnel are ill-equipped to handle its inmates. It has been unsuccessful in reducing crime or rehabilitating criminals. Until recently the courts have kept a "hands-off" doctrine permitting officials wide discretion with low visibility. It has been largely unresponsive to prisoners' and reform groups' claims for change. Finally, it has been near last on legislators' lists of priorities for modernization.

It has been necessary to elaborate in order to avoid a simplistic analysis of the question at hand, namely the prisoners' rights versus the public's rights. Frequently, such a discussion is seen through the prism of the zero-sum game where the gain for the one is automatically a loss—perhaps a total loss eventually—for the other. At the moment, extension of "rights" to prisoners is yielded grudgingly by administrators following public clamor, court orders, prison riots, and, less frequently, reform legislation. Very few corrections administrators plan the voluntary extension of rights to inmates. In professional correctional circles, most view this process as cataclysmic—a process which will some day produce a holocaust in the institutions.

It is the assumption of this paper that the extension and

elaboration of rights to the confined may be the more productive direction for corrections. It is a sad irony in our system of criminal justice that we insist on the full majesty of due process for the accused until he is sentenced to an institution and then justice is said to have been served. Consider that our penal codes make it mandatory that before a criminal sanction can be imposed, there be a finding beyond stringent levels of doubt that the accused's behavior was a union of *act* and *intent*—it was volitional. We will reduce degrees of responsibility for the alleged behavior if such behavior was nonvolitional. We are tough in standards of arrest, most stringent in the finding of guilt. The defendant is protected by the mantle of the presumption of innocence. The state must prove the allegations. The defendant may stand mute in court and is protected from conviction out of his own mouth. Anything brought before the court to support a prosecutor's claim can be challenged. We believe that this system is civilized and protects us all from star chamber injustices. The lowliest stands protected from the capriciousness of constituted authority.

The judicial subsystem is the most visible. It strains to protect the defendants by limiting the discretion of the judge to a finder of fact. The great irony occurs after a conviction when the judge commits a guilty offender to a prison. It takes a great flight of imagination or studied neglect to include the present correctional prison experience in a system of justice. The entire case for what can be called a *justice model* rests upon the need to continue to engage the person in the quest for justice as he moves on the continuum from defendant to convict to parolee.

The Justice Model

The theory of the justice model suggests that a fruitful way of teaching nonlaw abiders to be law abiding is to treat them in a lawful way, i.e., to bring the entire effort of the correctional agency into teaching lawful behavior by program and example.

The justice model would include efforts to place inmate populations and staff within a lawful and rational arena. Elements of this model for a prison would specifically, but not exhaustively, include:

1. Elements of self-governance
2. A system-wide ombudsman independent of the Department of Corrections
3. A law library
4. Civil legal assistance for indigent inmates
5. A prevailing-rate wage system in the prison industries
6. Opportunity to provide community service (a form of moral restitution)
7. Recognition of, and opportunity for, programming for different ethnic groups
8. Due procedural safeguards built into internal behavior management systems
9. No mail censorship
10. An extensive furlough program.
11. A contract system for parole with objectively possible criteria for progression through the incarceration experience
12. Introduction of adversary and appeal procedures into the parole revocation decision-making process
13. Open access of the correctional system to the press
14. A system of victim compensation and offender restitution

Other programs would include educational, recreational, vocational training, and industrial work opportunities. For those who wish to receive social work, psychological, and psychiatric services, a voucher system could be provided. A separate internal police force would be employed to enforce, when necessary, the explicated norms of this new prison society. Only a small part of the staff would have police functions, the major effort being carried by an internal nonuniformed counseling staff. This model purports to turn a prison experience into one which teaches and provides opportunities for men to learn to be agents in their own lives, to use legal processes to change their condition, and to wield lawful power. Men who can negotiate their fates do not have to turn to violence as a method of achieving change.

This strategy might provide the keeper and the kept with a rationale and morality for their shared fates in a correctional agency. Considering the failure of most treatment methods within our current operating structure—the fortress prison—the justice model holds some promise, if not to cut recidivism, then more decisively to preclude Atticas.

On one level we need a cultural reversal concerning the apparent attitude that the person convicted of a crime does not need or deserve further doses of justice. How else could the judicial dictum of the prisoner as a "slave of the state" have endured so long, accompanied quite appropriately by a judicial "hands-off" policy in relation to prison administration? In recent years it has become obvious that the "hands-off" policy is eroding. The timing for a reexamination of current styles and development of a new rationale for the prison experience is most propitious. It leads the way to engaging both the keeper and the kept in a manageable experience in prison. The keeper has always been at least as angry as the kept.

Our system of law insists, in effect, that it wants only volitional actors in the prison. Then it supports a treatment regimen which assumes nonvolitional behavior on the part of prisoners. The courts are increasingly aware of this dysfunctional aspect of the justice system and are responding by making themselves available as arbiters of predictable clashes between the keeper and the kept.

The proponents of the psychiatric or medical model of prisoner treatment visualized themselves as reformers. They grasped the prisoner from the onerous custody staff who merely meted out punishment for prison rule infractions. The clinicians viewed the prisoner as sick while custody staff saw them as bad. Both operated until most recently in an environment of low visibility and wide discretion—a sure formula for the distortion of justice in any social institution. But the convict, it appears, would rather be bad than sick. He can hang onto a soft determinism and still be volitional. The clinicians did not permit him much room for responsible behavior. One needs only to look at the extremes of either style to see their logical conclusions from Attica to Patuxent.

The justice model is based upon a rhetoric easily understood by the personnel who will be the dominant force in prisons for the foreseeable future—the custody staff. The guard can understand simple fairness and reasonableness. He can also understand the need to build structures to insure justice. Measuring prisoners' progress by their lawful behavior is as plausible to the guard as is measuring his own work progress and upward mobility by his lawful behavior.

Teaching inmates lawful behavior through lawful staff treatment and exposure of prisoners to lawful resources is not here proposed as a cry for "humanitarian" treatment for "oppressed" inmates. Rather, it is a reasoned response in the service of public safety. It is the "Realpolitik" of law and order.

The justice model seeks to engage both the keeper and the kept in a joint venture which insists that the agencies of justice shall operate in a lawful and just manner. It simply means that we believe that the prisoner did not use lawful means outside the prison and should therefore be provided greater (not fewer) opportunities to learn lawful behavior in the institution. The staff effort should be turned to teaching a prisoner how to use lawful processes to achieve his ends. This also implies responsibility for consequences of his behavior. In the absence of a continuum of justice in the prison, most ends are reached unlawfully. When unlawful behavior is detected, it is itself handled with the absence of the very standards of due process we insist upon outside the prison. The result is a further indication to the convict that lawful behavior for a convict has little pay-off. He can be dealt with arbitrarily and usually responds by treating others in the same manner. The justice model would make sure that the prisoner experienced lawful ways of dealing with problems with the expectation that there would be a carry-over to the point of release. The prison experience would try to guarantee that, at least for the period of incarceration, the prisoner would experience continual exposure to the type of life-style society expects him to pursue when he is released.

NORVAL MORRIS and MICHAEL MILLS

8. PRISONERS AS LABORATORY ANIMALS

Stateville Prison in Illinois might have been created by a Hollywood set designer. George Raft and his fellows in the romantic prison movies of the 1940s would recognize its massive walls looming over the empty countryside, the armed guard towers that prickle the horizon and the regimented flower beds at the front gate. Inside, the cells, exercise yards and vast steel-tabled dining halls would look familiar, too, although the occupants now are very much of the 1970s: young, mostly black, urban, violent and prone to riot.

Not a part of anyone's casual picture of prison life, then or now, is the Malaria Project located in a small research hospital in which Stateville prisoners serve as test subjects for new antimalarial drugs. Although Americans have largely forgotten the disease, save for a brief fever of interest in Vietnam, malaria remains the largest public health problem in the world: 200 million persons suffer each year and 2 million die. At Stateville, no one has died of malaria since the project began during World War II in a search for drugs to protect allied soldiers, but hundreds of prisoners have endured the fevers, chills and aches of the disease and many more have been dosed, measured, probed, punctured, wired and watched in other phases of the work.

Stateville is not alone in nurturing medical and other research. Prisoners make splendid laboratory animals. Healthy, relatively free of alcohol and drugs, with regulated diets, they are captives, unlikely to wander off and be lost to both treatment and

---

Norval Morris is Professor of Law and Director of the Center for Criminal Justice at the University of Chicago, and Michael Mills is a research associate at the same institution.

control groups, and they are under sufficient pressure of adversity to "volunteer." No one knows precisely how many prisoners are sampling drugs, ingesting food additives or swabbing themselves with cosmetics. Reflecting a widespread lack of any but punitive interest in our prison systems, we do not know who or how many or where our guinea pigs are, the risks to which they are exposed, the rewards they receive or the conditions of their consent.

Nevertheless our investigations—and those of Walter Rugaber and Jessica Mitford before us—have marked out the range and character of research in prisons. Somewhat unfashionably in disagreement with Mitford and other liberal reformers of the prisons, we are persuaded that research in prisons can with appropriate safeguards make a useful contribution to the prisoner's welfare, to reform of the correctional system and, not least, to medical progress. We found research of four kinds:

1. Testing methods of treating prisoners to "cure" their criminality,
2. Testing new drugs for pharmaceutical manufacturers,
3. Engaging in medical research not related to drugs,
4. Testing cosmetics, hand lotions, band-aids and the like.

We do not in this study mark out the moral limits on coercively curing criminals. B. F. Skinner and *A Clockwork Orange,* aversive conditioning and *The Terminal Man* demand a complex inquiry into the foundations of criminal punishment, a task beyond our ambitions here. We do believe, however, that examining the use of prisoners in medical and quasi-medical research, for public health as distinct from crime-control purposes, will provide first approximations of the answers to the broader inquiry. First, therefore, we address the prisoner's role in drug testing.

Human Guinea Pigs

Drugs for humans are tested in three stages after animal studies are complete. In Phase I, the new compound is given to fewer than 100 normal, healthy persons in order to measure absorption, bioavailability, toxicity and side effects. Anyone can be a Phase I test subject; he need not have or risk the condition to be treated. As one researcher put it to us, "I've never tested in prisons, but I'm always looking for good subjects. Hell, I tested a contraceptive on a flock of nuns." He meant Phase I testing, to be sure, since in Phase II the drug's *effectiveness* is tested for the first time on a small group of patients. Prisoners excel in Phase I tests and, according to Dr. Marion Finkel, deputy director of the FDA's Bureau of Drugs, do "virtually all" such work for the drug industry.

Prisoners may also be Phase II subjects. At Stateville, for example, testing antimalarial drugs requires that disease-carrying mosquitoes be given an occasional free lunch upon a dozen or so healthy prisoners. That feeding ensures a supply of "patients" in a nation to which malaria is now virtually unknown.

If the drug appears safe and effective, testing moves into Phase III or controlled field trials involving as many as 5,000 patients. Antimalarial compounds are shipped to doctors in Southeast Asia, Latin America and other areas of the world where malaria is endemic. There, the new drugs are given to patients in the course of regular—but carefully observed—medical treatment. These stages are suggested by their apparent scientific logic and mandated by the Food and Drug Administration since 1962 when the European thalidomide tragedies moved Congress to require more extensive proof of new drug safety as well as efficacy.

Darvon, a product of Eli Lilly and Company, is one of the most common drugs for, as the package insert states, "the relief of mild to moderate pain." One of its forms, Darvon-N, was extensively tested in Phase I by prisoners of the Indiana State Reformatory, a part of the Indiana prison system with which Lilly has a close and symbiotic relationship. At the Lilly Laboratory for Clinical Research in the Marion County General Hospital in Indianapolis, a special ward has been established for Phase I testing. As many as 16 inmates at a time, selected from a long waiting list that has been screened by the prison staff, will be transferred from the reformatory to the hospital for three to six weeks of research participation.

Last year 77 men came from the reformatory to the Lilly laboratory as research subjects. What did they get? They got a ward without guards as well as cigarettes, books, barbering, craft and hobby materials, color television, exercise rooms, daily rather than biweekly visiting privileges and $2 per day. (In the prison, regular wages are 20 cents per day, and there are no color televisions.) They also get the chance to make at least a small choice about their own lives in an otherwise wholly regimented setting. In turn the prison got a dishwasher, a remodeled hospital, high school supplies, an improved library and athletic equipment. And, of course, Lilly got its Phase I test results.

Lilly also conducts research with prisoners in the reformatory hospital and at the Marion County Jail, using nearly 1,000 men at the reformatory and 42 at the jail last year. In another mutually beneficial arrangement the Upjohn and Parke-Davis companies do their testing at the Southern Michigan State Prison at Jackson. Well over $1 million has been invested in sophisticated research clinics through which nearly half of the prison's 5,000 population pass each year. In addition to paying the prisoners on an elaborate schedule that ranges from 25 cents for a fingertip blood sample to $12 for a spinal tap, Upjohn provides pharmacy services and some emergency equipment to the prison's hospital. Moreover, the process of screening the volunteers often reveals medical problems that are referred to prison physicians for treatment.

Not all prison testing of new drugs is done with the scientific rigor and medical sophistication that Lilly, Upjohn and Parke-Davis plainly apply to their work in Indiana and Michigan. Many drug companies contract for research with individual physicians, university hospitals, clinics and profit-making firms. The nature and extent of this farmed-out work is known only to the FDA, and only dimly to that agency. Dr. Alan Lisook, of the FDA's Office of Scientific Evaluation, told us that records of test sites are not routinely kept and could be obtained only by laboriously searching through each of the approximately 1,000 new drug applications filed every year.

One man whose work for drug manufacturers became well known is Dr. Austin Stough, an Oklahoma physician who left a trail of hepatitis and corruption through the prison systems of several states. His firm, Southern Food and Drug Research, virtually bought control of the Alabama prisons, reaping profits by testing drugs and selling blood plasma. Walter Rugaber's 1969 stories in the *New York Times* revealed that many of Stough's tests were scientifically worthless and medically irresponsible, but evidently not enough so to trouble either the sponsoring manufacturers (among them Wyeth Laboratories and Merck, Sharp & Dohme) or the FDA. A committee of the Alabama Medical Association reported that the manufacturers had "demonstrated some lack of discretion" in failing to supervise adequately the work upon which their claims of safety and efficacy for new drugs were to be based. Prisoners were not given proper examinations, many failed to take prescribed doses of the drugs and at Kilby Prison near Montgomery the hospital director was "a man with very little previous medical training whose experience . . . had been that of a venereal disease inspector."

Although the drug-testing programs were unsound and dangerous to potential consumers of new drugs, the prisoners suffered most from Stough's plasmapheresis project. In a variation of usual blood donation, a unit of blood is extracted, the plasma separated and the rest is reinjected into the donor—as often as 16 times a month. This procedure is not experimental, but was conducted with gross indifference to infection of the donors from contaminated apparatus and unsterile procedures. There, an epidemic of more than 500 cases of serum hepatitis, three of them fatal, went unnoticed.

In his busiest years, the mid-1960s Dr. Stough was responsible for between 25 and 50 percent of all Phase I testing in the country and supplied 25 percent of the blood plasma. Now that he is dead, the FDA has issued regulations requiring that all drug testing be reviewed by independent committees of scientists, but in the absence of effective FDA supervision we have little assurance that another such grotesquerie will not soon be uncovered in another prison.

We also found medical research in prisons not related either to curing criminals or to testing drugs. Infectious hepatitis is a mild disease (unlike the dangerous serum hepatitis associated with addicts' needles and commercial blood banks) but so common that 9 out of 10 children will have it by the time they are 10 years old. The nature of the transmitting agent and the pattern of infectiousness are not understood. Awkwardly for researchers, rats and cats and other usual laboratory animals refuse to become infected. Even marmosets have been tried but only humans will do—and they must be in isolation to avoid uncontrolled exposure to infection.

Dr. Joseph Boggs of Northwestern University Medical School told us that he would be more afraid of measles than infectious hepatitis, but has suspended his studies on prisoners because recent political attention has made the research climate tense. The *New York Times* report of the abuses of Tuskegee, where hundreds of syphilis victims were left untreated in the name of science, and the revelations by Jessica Mitford in an *Atlantic* article have led all researchers to rethink questions of human rights. In the words of Gerald Houlihan of the New York State Department of Corrections, "Tuskegee scared the hell out of prison people." But, Dr. Boggs said, a ban on work in prisons "will absolutely stop research on hepatitis."

At the Oregon State Penitentiary, eight men some years ago subjected themselves to bilateral testicular biopsies as part of an investigation in reproductive health. The doctors wanted to know whether certain drugs would affect the rate of sperm production. Under local anesthesia, small incisions were made through which tissue was removed for examination, both before and after administration of steroids and sex hormones. To what result? As the doctors put it, "the rate of spermatogenesis in man therefore appears to be a biological constant in confirmation of Ortavant's conclusion derived from . . . studies on the ram."

The fourth kind of research in which prisoners are involved flows from America's insistent demand for shiny hair, processed food and sure cosmetic happiness. The shampoo that won't make baby cry was tested on a group of healthy and not particularly lachrymose adult prisoners. Sweeteners, expanders, smoothers, fresheners, brighteners, preservatives and other chemicals of the food industry must also be checked for safety: prisoners gulp them in massive doses. Miracle ingredients for face creams and wrinkle removers must pass a mundane test to be sure they are harmless (their efficacy being left for consumers to judge), and that too occurs in prison.

Hill Top Research, a private laboratory, uses prisoners from the Indiana State Prison in a variety of tests. Some are Phase I tests done under contract to drug manufacturers, but most are less exotic. For example, 210 men last year used new deodorant soaps for 10 days, allowing the investigators to make olfactory tests of the soaps' effectiveness. Another 200 men spent 15 days buttering themselves with a palette of cosmetics, soaps, perfumes and antiperspirants—to test for irritation and sensitivity. Similarly, a surgical scrub soap was checked for its ability to remove skin bacteria.

Jack Wild, Hill Top's vice-president, enthusiastically informed us that his firm does more testing outside prisons than in, often working with church and other volunteer groups that want to raise money. For nondrug tests, in which precise control and minute observation are less critical, free subjects are as good as prisoners.

A Question of Freedom

Prisoners are, it is clear, extensively used as the objects of drug and medical research, ranging from the vital to the frivolous. Should they be? Are they appropriate laboratory animals? Can a prisoner volunteer? Can he consent? Is not *free* consent by a prisoner a contradiction in terms?

The Declaration of Helsinki was the postwar medical world's formal reaction to the revelations at Nuremberg of Nazi abuse of prisoners in monstrous medical experiments. The declaration, when first drafted, contained a ban on the use of all prisoners in medical research. In its present form it forbids the use only of "administrative and political prisoners." The ethical basis of this distinction is at least elusive.

English, European and some American correctional administrators adhere to the earlier Helsinki position that prison life is inherently coercive and for this reason prohibit research using prisoners. The Oregon State Penitentiary, site of the testicular biopsy study described earlier, no longer permits medical research on its inmates. Administrator Hoyt Cupp told us that he had made the decision to ban research because "We're not running a Greek democracy here; no man is a free agent in prison."

Such a ban no doubt impedes medical progress important to the patient and the professional. More Asians and Africans would die from malaria without continued research, and England's strict control of animal vivisection and human subject research has, in the words of one medical commentator, made her "a second-rate biomedical power." America demands premarket testing, but that requires healthy, willing subjects, usually prisoners. Other nations are less demanding, but patients who get new drugs bear greater risks. The balance between medical progress and respect for human integrity is uneasy.

Asked about the consequences of a ban on research in prisons, Alan Lisook of the FDA said to us, "It would probably be disastrous. Our criteria for the approval of drugs, the amount of testing we require, are very strict. The British get along without prisoners, but they do not have such tough standards." He cautioned, however, that "it is obvious they're not dropping like flies in Britain."

Carrying our search for alternative test subjects to doctors running these experiments in prison, our inquiry "How many prison staff have volunteered?" was not well received. We hesitated to mention Jessica Mitford's trenchant suggestion that stockholders of drug companies would be the ideal voluntary subjects. Before being swept along by radical enthusiasm, however, it is well to recognize that prisoners themselves would deeply resent a ban on, as they see it, their freedom to volunteer. They need the money and they want to be of use to the community. Indeed, in April of last year 96 of the 175 inmates of the Lancaster County Pennsylvania Prison wrote to the local newspaper protesting the state's decision to stop all medical experiments on state prisoners, including the antibiotic research at Lancaster. The disgruntled prisoners made the points that they were unharmed and that the project allowed them to pay off their fines and court costs.

Absolutist positions are seductive but have at least two defects: they are unlikely to be accepted and, granting the need for human experimental subjects, it would seem a pity to exclude prisoners from participation if their involvement can be made advantageous both to them and to the community. So the contour lines of an *unfree,* informed, ethically justified consent must be sketched. The problem is one of coercion, the relationship between the effects of captivity and the ethics of consent.

Coercion diffuses along a troublesome continuum. Ivan Denisovitch would eagerly volunteer for a drug test merely to escape the Siberian cold for a day; add a crust of bread and the inducement would be overpowering. By constrast, in a small, open prison, decently run and containing short-term prisoners, there will be no stampede to participate.

At the Texas State Penitentiary in Hunstville, researchers from the Baylor College of Medicine and from the University of Texas carry on studies of respiratory diseases and cholera vaccines involving several hundred men per year. The inmates are paid $5 for each day's research participation, but nothing at all for work in the prison. The studies get many more volunteers than they can use; nonetheless, Carl Jeffries, director of support services for the Texas Department of Corrections, did not appear disturbed. He told us that, "We do not coerce these men in any way, shape, or form."

In Vermont, the state prison is now called the State Correctional Facility and holds only 140 men, half its 1969 population. The others have been transferred to small community correctional centers and have so reduced the volunteer pool that a long-term study of the relationship between obesity and diabetes had to be terminated for lack of subjects. Warden J. V. Moeykens, whose voice carries little of the tension heard in the voices of America's megaprison wardens, said when we asked about future research possibilities, "I would discourage them. Our first job here is corrections, and I just don't have the space to give up to outside projects." Warden Moeykens may be right, but there are clear advantages to the prison system in the presence of the medical researcher. He tends to inhibit otherwise hidden brutalities and to reduce the social isolation of the prison. In the sense that the prison institution tries to keep responsible community influences out, the medical research team breaks down the walls.

Rewards of Research

Why do prisoners volunteer? Freud is right, human behavior is overdetermined; here as elsewhere is a multiplicity of motives. Machismo, which leads prisoners to exaggerate the risks they take, is one. The altruism of community service is another, carrying with it for the prisoner the assurance that he is as virtuous as those outside who have banished and rejected him. And if he sees himself as having wronged others by his crimes, here is a chance for expiation, of making restitution. Psychopathology apart, prisoners seem to be persistent risk takers—as their presence in prison suggests.

Other motives are obvious and less noble: the hope of earlier release, the reward of payment. These two merit closer consideration. But there is also one strong complex of pressures on the prisoner that is less well known. Participation in experiments provides an immediate temporary escape from the pervasive fear, endemic brutality and total anonymity of the typical American megaprison. When we visited Stateville, nearly 40 men were in solitary because they had asked to be—for their own safety.

These pressures are, if anything, even stronger in overcrowded city jails, many of which are also involved in drug tests. Jail life is unstable, no other jobs are available and the need for money in the jail and as a stake upon release is even more compelling. Most prisoners are locked up in a jail, after all, solely because they lack money for a bail bond.

Inmates of state and federal prisons know that the fact of their volunteering for medical experiments is noted on the records seen by the parole board. But they do not deceive themselves that volunteering has more than marginal influence on their chances for parole. Prisoners tend to see parole decisions as so capricious and unprincipled that participation in medical experiments cannot be a reliable key to unlock the prison gates. A temporary escape to a less brutal imprisonment, yes—but a sure path to an early freedom, certainly not.

Nathan Leopold, of the Loeb and Leopold case, an early volunteer for the Stateville Malaria Project, put it well: "There was no assurance whatever that volunteers would be rewarded by having their time cut. Of that fact each group was solemnly and emphatically reminded before they were allowed to sign their contracts. But the possibility did exist that there would be time cuts. And that was a chance I could not afford to miss."

What of the economic incentive? The usual payment is toward the top of the prison wage scale, say $1 or $1.50 a day. Those of us on the outside may not find $1.50 either sufficient reward or compelling incentive, but our economic choices are not so restricted, nor are our markets so deflated. One prisoner reminded us that the state's grant to him upon discharge will be $50, "enough to buy a gun and a few bullets." A longtime participant in the Stateville Malaria Project, he will instead take with him about $300 in accumulated research pay, enough, he says, "to make a fair stake for a new start."

There is a dilemma here. If we offer the prisoner what would be necessary to attract the next less vulnerable group, say the free unemployed, then the effect of this payment in the prison marketplace will be unacceptably coercive. But if we do not, it is plain that the prisoner is being used to subsidize the drug company and the medical researcher. Although for some researchers subject costs may be important, the large pharmaceutical companies are not troubled by paying substantially more than they now do. We should perhaps note, as did Dr. James Goddard, former chief of the FDA, that the pharmaceutical industry has a higher rate of return on its capital investment than any other industry in America. Dr. Alan Varley, medical director of Upjohn, informed us that, "The development cost of a new drug may be $7 million: what we pay prisoner subjects is an insignificant part of that total. We would like to pay more, but prison administrators won't let us."

In searching for alternatives it may help to consider the practice of using prisoners in a less emotionally charged but analogous setting. Occasionally in country districts near a prison there will be a shortage of labor to harvest a crop. Prisoners will volunteer to help; promises not to try to escape will be extracted and cautiously evaluated; and teams of prisoners will bring in the crop. The proper economic arrangements have evolved in many parts of the world to meet this common contingency. The farmer pays the cost of an ordinary farm laborer and the prisoners receive the top of the prison wage scale. The substantial difference is held in trust by the prison administrator for prisoner welfare. Larger stakes on release for all prisoners might be one socially sensible use for these funds.

But prison is a potently corruptive institution and even this arrangement has resonances of corruption. Stories of brutal jailers selling prison labor and pocketing the proceeds, of the economic serfdom achieved in the early English jails under private franchise, of southern chain gangs at work on private farms come to mind. Most state prison systems are rife with rumor, and perhaps fact, about misappropriation of prisoner funds by staff. Any unsupervised system can be abused.

At the present stage of penal development in this country, the surplus value of the prisoner's labor as a volunteer for medical research, the product of the apparent arbitrage between the captive and free labor markets should be held to the benefit of prisoners generally. The prisoner subsidization of drug companies and medical research is inequitable and unprincipled, encouraging the manipulation of economically vulnerable people.

If, as seems desirable, we dramatically change the character of our prisons, arrangements different and better than the welfare fund we have proposed could be made. A presidential task force recommended the establishment of a full wages prison on an experimental basis. The prisoner would be compensated at the ordinary market rates for his labor and would meet the costs of his board and keep (not of his imprisonment—that is what we and he pay taxes for). Similarly, the National Council on Crime and Delinquency is urging that private enterprise take over prison production, establishing rates of remuneration and standards of safety applicable to free industry and manufacture. Under such practices, the prisoner's involvement in medical research would present no economic problem—he would receive the free market rate.

It is clearly improper to require, as some projects do, that volunteers sign waivers of their right to sue for damages for injuries or illness flowing from negligence in the conduct of the experiment. It is doubtful that such waivers are binding; in any event they are unethical. But that is not enough. The prison volunteer must be compensated for any medical expenses or loss of earning capacity by the experiment. We need, in effect, "no fault" liability here, too. The prisoner may properly volunteer to bear the physical risk, but he should not be expected to volunteer to bear the economic risk.

There is no great cost in this. Such lasting illnesses are rare indeed—in the 25 years of the malaria project at Stateville Prison, Illinois, not one has occurred. The dangers are much less than those in other prison trades and industries. The entrepreneurs of research should ensure against such costs or perhaps special funds like workmen's compensation might be established. The Illinois General Assembly is now considering legislation drafted by one of the authors that would assure compensation for all human subjects, captive and free alike.

We are, of course, assuming that any research done in prisons has been subject to the professional peer review required of virtually all research. Senator Edward M. Kennedy has proposed a National Commission for the Protection of Human Subjects, with wide authority to regulate research. One part of that proposal replaces existing peer review committees with an institutional human investigation committee (IHIC). IHIC would serve as liaison between the research institution and the National Commission and would have two subcommittees: a protocol review group (PRG) made up of research professionals and a subject advisory group (SAG) to control and review procedures for obtaining informed consent.

Whether or not SAGs would be useful generally is problematic. It is hard to see any commonality among, for example, patients in a general hospital that would make them effective and critical members of a subject advisory group. But the idea is excellent for prisons and prisoners. In each prison or jail the SAG should include prisoners as a majority of its members, preferably other than those who are participating, have participated or hope to participate as subjects of medical research. Professional peer group review can assure an appropriate benefit/risk ratio, examine research protocols and certain aspects of informing potential volunteers. Prisoner advisory group review will help to achieve decency in the difficult issues of informed and free consent in captivity and the economic aspects of volunteering when destitute.

The Department of Health, Education and Welfare, which funds much research and regulates all drug testing, early in 1974 proposed new regulations governing the use of prisoners in activities within the agency's jurisdiction. If they are adopted, they will have nearly universal application, because most institutions and firms conducting non-HEW activities are also engaged in HEW work and have a single set of procedures for both. .

The regulations provide that no federally funded research or testing of drugs for FDA approval be conducted unless the prison meets federal standards for medical care, living conditions, alternative work opportunities and wage levels. A review committee, one of whose members shall be a prisoner or "a representative of an organization having as a primary concern protection of the interests of prisoners," will review procedures for selection of participants and monitor the conduct of research.

HEW intends to accredit prisons for research if they comply with the regulations and have adequate facilities. We are not certain what the effect of these new regulations will be, though the intention and the policy statement are laudable. If prisons shut out researchers because of unwillingness to improve their facilities, then inmates will have lost the benefits we think come from this work. If HEW accredits institutions without serious investigation because manpower is as insufficient for this task as it already is for inspection of drug-testing programs generally, then unacceptable programs will have acquired a protective imprimatur. Finally, we do not think the proposals go far enough: the pay differential problem is not addressed.

Discussion about the use of prisoners in research usually turns into a conflict between the dignity and integrity of the individual on one hand and the freedom of scientific inquiry on the other. That argument is too easily lost in rhetorical foliage. What we must face is that prisoners want to participate, that flat bans may drive more testing overseas to countries less scrupulous (presumably because less wealthy) about the use of human subjects and that the free consent of the unfree *can* be protected.

We do not say that existing protections are adequate; obviously, they are not. Rather, we have asserted that no insurmountable barrier to participation lies either in the ethics of consent or in the quality of prison life.

In our view, three things must be done if prisoners are to continue to be used as laboratory animals:

1. Prisoners must be paid what would be required to attract a free volunteer to the same research project. So long as internal prison wages are low, the difference between the low prison wage and a free volunteer's reward must be paid into a fund for the general welfare of prisoners.

2. Any prison permitting research must establish, in addition to a scientific review group, a subject advisory group, a majority of whose members are prisoners.

3. Prisoners must be compensated for all lasting injury or loss of earnings suffered as a result of participation in a research project.

With these minimum safeguards as a precondition to the ethical participation of this vulnerable group, we believe that medical research in prisons can be beneficial to society, to the prison system and to the prisoner himself. Without them, we must agree with philosopher Hans Jonas that "society would indeed be threatened by the erosion of those moral values whose loss, possibly caused by too ruthless a pursuit of scientific progress, would make its most dazzling triumphs not worth having."

IV

NEW DIRECTIONS
FOR CRIMINAL JUSTICE

GERALD M. CAPLAN

9. NEW DIRECTIONS IN CRIMINAL JUSTICE RESEARCH

I appreciate this opportunity to present some of the new directions in criminal justice research we are charting at the National Institute of Law Enforcement and Criminal Justice.

As the research center of the Law Enforcement Assistance Administration, the Institute's mandate is to challenge the conventional wisdom of the day, to test current assumptions about crime prevention and control, and to find out what works and what does not work. The same progress that has been made through research in other areas—health, defense, space—can be made in the field of criminal justice.

Although advances have occurred in recent years, particularly since the creation of LEAA in 1968, the fact is that we are still wrestling with the fundamentals: What are the causes of crime? How should we handle those who have broken the law? How do we deter those who might do so in the future?

Our research continues at a particularly difficult time. Confidence in the criminal justice system—indeed, in government at all levels—seems low. In criminal justice, we are learning that much of the problem lies with the way the average citizen is treated when he comes into contact with the system as a witness, juror, or victim. For many citizens, victimization continues after the crime has occurred. Often their needs and problems are ignored, and they are treated poorly by those charged with helping them. A system designed to aid them becomes the enemy.

Recent LEAA-sponsored surveys of crime victims indicate

Gerald M. Caplan is Director of the National Institute of Law Enforcement of the Law Enforcement Assistance Administration, in the Department of Justice.

that large numbers of citizens fail to report crimes, even the most serious ones. In a survey of the nation's five largest cities, we found that unreported crime is two to three times as high as reported crime in Chicago, Detroit, Los Angeles, and New York. And, in Philadelphia, the actual crime rate is five times higher than reported crime.

Of course, the phenomenon of unreported crime is not in itself surprising. Surveys conducted for the President's Crime Commission in the mid-sixties found that many crimes are never reported to the police. Even without the benefit of these surveys, experts have long suspected that there was much unreported crime. But few believed that it was of the proportions revealed by the recent National Crime Panel.

Of those who did not report crimes against them, how many lacked enough confidence in our criminal justice agencies to seek their assistance? How many were so turned off by the system and its maze of legalisms and procedures that permanent loss and silent suffering seemed preferable? A great many, we suspect. The most common reasons for not reporting crimes, according to the National Crime Panel, were that the victims felt the police "couldn't do anything" or the incident "wasn't important enough."

The problem cries out for attention. Concern for the crime victim should match concern for the offender. Yet the millions now spent studying the problems of offenders dramatically outweigh the meager sums allocated to the problems of victims, witnesses, and jurors. Our creative energies and funding priorities need to be redirected to reflect this concern.

The Institute is giving priority to efforts to gain a better understanding of citizen concerns and to programs to build a more responsive criminal justice system.

New Directions for the Courts

Many victims are simply worn out by a certain type of legal maneuvering called plea bargaining. In our system, plea bargaining is the rule—not the exception. It is an affair between the accused and the government. It excludes the person most concerned with the crime and its outcome: the victim. Consequently, many victims, rightly or not, see this negotiation process as proof that justice for them has been denied.

As part of the Institute's victim studies, we are investigating the feasibility of involving the victim in the plea-bargaining process, perhaps at a pretrial conference, presided over by a judge. The victim—possibly through counsel—would be given the opportunity to have a say, to participate in the eventual bargained decision.

This would be, of course, a radical departure from traditional practice. It may not work; certainly its implications are not fully understood. But we think it merits examination.

Creation of a victim ombudsman is another idea that may have merit. The ombudsman would be a court officer assigned to help victims, to keep them informed of the progress of their cases. He would explain the various steps in the criminal process and give the victim a more realistic understanding of the law and of what is expected of him. This would be preferable to existing procedures whereby the victim only knows what is going on when he gets hit by a subpoena ordering him to appear in court or suffer dire consequences if he does not.

Another study will address the crime of rape, where the attitude of policemen and prosecutors—and doctors—has such a profound and often negative effect on the victim. The Institute is researching the ways in which rape victims and witnesses are treated in police stations, hospitals, and courtrooms, and will suggest improvements to increase the victim's willingness to testify against her assailant.

Victim compensation and offender reparation plans are also on our agenda. Several proposals have been made in this area: public or private insurance, restitution as a condition of probation, fines, part of which go directly to the victim, or attachment of prison earnings to be paid as reparation to the victim. These, among others, may provide better assistance to those whom we have been unable to protect from crime.

Our neglect is not confined to victims alone. There are serious problems in securing the cooperation of witnesses. Too many witnesses to crimes simply will not help the police or prosecution. They will not come to court.

An Institute-sponsored study of witnesses in the District of Columbia gives some indication of the scope of the problem. Preliminary data show that of nearly 8,000 cases presented for prosecution during the first half of 1973, about 3,000 cases were rejected, nolle prossed, or dismissed. The reason in 42 percent of the cases was that witnesses would not cooperate.

Citizen witnesses are not the only people who suffer from the courts' inefficiencies. The Commissioner of the Highway Patrol in a major state reported that his men spent 60 percent of their court time just waiting—a total of 400,000 lost man-hours in one year. Local police departments in the same state reported that as much as 85 percent of their officers' court time was similarly spent—waiting. A study in one medium-sized city showed that, in 70 percent of the cases in which an officer was summoned to appear in court, he was *never even called to testify.* The citizen pays again: the 10 billion dollars it costs to run the criminal justice system comes out of his pocket.

Jurors face comparable problems. In one major city jurors reportedly spent up to 62 percent of their time in the waiting room. It is common knowledge that the atmosphere of the average jury waiting room can quickly dampen the ardor of even the most civic-minded person.

The Institute has just completed a study of jury operations in seven state and local courts of general jurisdiction. The project found that criminal court jury pools can be cut by 20 to 25 percent and still provide adequate numbers of jurors for trials. If these results hold true nationally—and we strongly suspect that they do—this would save the taxpayers as much as $50 million each year. Equally important, dissatisfaction of those called to duty would be minimized.

A recent news report illustrates the frustration faced by many jurors. After serving only twenty days in a three-month period, a Detroit housewife angrily told the trial judge that jurors were herded around like animals, were never told what was happening, and spent most of their time waiting, not knowing what they were waiting for. She concluded: "If I ever get in trouble,

I'll never ask for a jury trial. I don't want to be judged by a group of angry, frustrated people."

Another subject that troubles citizens is excessive court delay. They do not understand why it takes so long for a verdict to be rendered. In our quest for individualized justice, with the very elaborate process of grand juries, preliminary hearings, arraignments and prolonged appeals, it sometimes appears that we have so overloaded the system that we are getting no justice at all. Has the search for a fair trial been replaced by the search for the perfect trial?

Streamlining pretrial procedures is one answer. One National Institute project, conducted by the Case Western Reserve University Law School, recommended twenty-five procedural changes to reduce pretrial delay, including limitations on pretrial proceedings, improved booking and bail procedures, increased use of pretrial conferences, limitations in the use of grand juries, consolidation of motions, and other organizational and administrative recommendations. This year, under a follow-up grant, the recommendations are being tested in three cities—New Haven, Norfolk, and Salt Lake City. When completed, the project will publish a guide for reducing court delay suitable for distribution to every urban court system in the country.

Another approach to reducing delay is to minimize the amount of time courts must spend on minor cases, some of which may not belong in the courts at all. In some urban criminal courts, 80 to 90 percent of the caseloads are traffic cases. Of California's 1,133 judges, 600—over half—hear traffic cases. Diversion of minor traffic offenses from the criminal justice system may be the solution. In June 1970, half of the 150,000 cases pending before the New York City Criminal Courts were traffic cases. Many had been pending for a year or more. New York transferred nonmisdemeanor moving traffic offenses—speeding, disobeying signs or signals, violating rights of way, improper turning and passing—from the criminal courts to the Motor Vehicle Department's Administrative Adjudication Bureau. At the end of the first operational year, department hearing officers had processed more than 560,000 complaints, conducted more than 180,000 hearings and revoked or suspended some 2,000 driver licenses. Cases were disposed of within four to six weeks, far more quickly than in the criminal court system.

More important, the decriminalization of all but the most serious traffic offenses would reflect the public view that running a red light is less serious than an assault. Why go out of our way to treat the average citizen as a common criminal?

The Institute will evaluate the experience of jurisdictions using administrative procedures for traffic offenses, and, if these look promising, move on to develop planning guidelines for interested jurisdictions.

New Directions for Police

For most citizens, the police are the most visible representatives of the criminal justice system. They are usually the first summoned in a sudden crisis. Police have a swift response capability and they have the authority—both legal and symbolic—to "do something."

We know, however, that many calls for police intervention arise from personal crises where an arrest may be inappropriate or unnecessary and yet these cries for help deserve a meaningful response.

Given proper training, the police have a unique potential to alleviate or prevent violence and to deal effectively with serious citizen problems.

Several years ago, the Institute financed a project which developed crisis intervention training to equip police to deal with family conflicts.

A major purpose of the project was to increase police safety, since intervening in family quarrels is one of the policeman's most hazardous assignments. In the Institute-funded project, injuries to crisis-trained police and the families they assisted were substantially reduced.

The project had more far-reaching implications than improved safety, however. The Family Crisis Intervention concept changes the police function in concrete and positive ways. Success is measured in terms of police ability to solve disputes rather than piling up felony arrests. The long-term results should be fewer arrests for family fights—and more lives of police officers saved.

Prisons

Today, we are in the midst of a strong trend away from maximum security institutions in rural areas to various forms of community-based corrections. Many argue that prisons are on the way out. The feeling is that it is not possible to humanize prisons, and that if we are to rehabilitate offenders we must first tear down the walls.

Many laud the efforts to put an end to "fortress prisons" and the repressive concepts they are said to represent. But a word of caution is in order. We do not want to be like the planner who designed a model city but neglected to provide for a cemetery. In our zeal to rehabilitate, we do not want to lose sight of the modesty of the tools at our disposal. Despite all our hopes, there will always be a need to incarcerate some offenders because they have hurt their neighbors, and because we do not have the slightest idea how to teach them not to do so again in the future.

Apart from any notion of rehabilitation or treatment, there is the deeply-held view, felt particularly with regard to white collar and upper-income offenders, that they have forfeited their right to associate in a civil society. We put them away not to help them but to punish them and to pronounce to the world that they have done wrong. These pronouncements are symbolic statements of great importance. They reflect our deepest values about right and wrong, and, to some degree, they avoid the greater evil of private retribution.

Of course, there are offenders that we do rehabilitate—at least as measured by lowered recidivism. We don't know exactly how it happens, but many institutionalized offenders are not rearrested after release. The Federal Bureau of Prisons recently disclosed the findings of a study of 1,800 inmates released from Federal prisons during 1970. The success rate for prisoners released or paroled was 67 percent. In other words, two out of every three offenders released continued to live in the community without having been convicted of a serious crime within two years of their release.

Another arresting finding of the Bureau of Prisons study is that inmates in the system today are more likely to have committed serious crimes than inmates of ten or fifteen years ago. In Dr. Daniel Glaser's study of the Federal system in 1956, 11 percent of the inmates that year had been convicted of such serious crimes as homicide, kidnapping, extortion, robbery, assault, and narcotics trafficking. In 1970, 15 percent of the inmates were convicted of these crimes. Although the inmates have gotten tougher, the success rate has improved, according to the Federal study.

This is not to suggest that this study proves that prison rehabilitation programs work, or that they work better than other programs based in urban settings. But it is fair to suppose that some ex-convicts gained something from the experience, if only a measure of fear or prudence that keeps them from breaking the law again. The interesting question is not so much the statistical one—how many recidivate?—but the qualitative one: which prisoners recidivate, which ones do not and why? Before consigning prisons to the historic preservationists, it would be wise to know a little more.

These observations are not intended to disparage efforts at reform. These must continue. We at LEAA spend millions of dollars every year supporting them. But at the same time, it may be appropriate to temper enthusiasm for specific reforms before they are evaluated.

The Institute is supporting a major study of current correctional theory and programming which we hope will provide some of the sound data we need. The Reconceptualization of Adult Corrections project will explore the philosophical underpinnings on which correctional programs are based, to determine the extent to which they are borne out by empirical data, and chart new directions for future research.

In recognition of the trend away from traditional incarceration towards community-based treatment centers, the project will devote major attention to evaluation of community-based services. Another Institute project will attempt to provide information on the costs of correctional reforms. Often new programs are adopted before we realize the demand they place on scarce resources. Or the economies of a promising approach may not be immediately apparent and an opportunity for constructive change may be missed.

Under the Institute grant, the American Bar Association, through its newly formed Correctional Economics Center, will analyze the recommendations for corrections improvements made by the National Advisory Commission on Criminal Justice Standards and Goals. The project will develop cost estimates to help correctional planners and administrators make informed decisions.

New Directions in Crime Prevention

Crime reduction is a difficult, complex task—one that cannot be accomplished solely by criminal justice agencies. A new and promising avenue to crime prevention was opened up through the pioneering work of the National Institute in environmental design. Institute research projects have developed physical planning principles which can enhance the safety of a building or neighborhood.

In 1969, an Institute grant to Oscar Newman of New York University began the landmark research into the relationship bewteen architectural design and crime prevention which culminated in the concept of defensible space. Analyzing over 100 housing projects across the country, the research identified four critical design elements that increase safety: First, the subdivision of public space into strongly defined zones of territorial influence. The fewer people who use a hall or door, the more protective their attitude toward it and one another. Second, the creation of opportunities for natural surveillance through the placement of doors, lobbies and windows. The knowledge—by both resident and intruder—that they can be seen constantly can allay fear and deter crime. Third, the removal of the stigma of an institutional appearance. Finally, recognition that the character of the surrounding neighborhood affects the safety of the project's public areas.

We now know that dramatic differences in crime rates are related to building design. In the Institute project, two adjacent housing projects in New York City were studied. Similar in size, density, and population make-up, they differed only in design. One was anonymous high-rise slabs and the other small, walk-up buildings where residents knew each other. The high-rise building had 66 percent more total crime, almost three times as many robberies, and 60 percent more felonies and misdemeanors. Police and tenants both reported a more friendly, effective relationship in the smaller buildings.

Environmental design, however, involves more than simply redesigning spatial relations. Properly performed, it changes the residents' use of and attitude toward their "territory." The Institute recently awarded 2 million dollars for a program to extend these design concepts to residential areas, commercial sections, schools and public transportation systems.

Brighter streets are generally assumed by the public to be safer streets. This assumption is shared by many law enforcement and municipal officials and has led a number of communities to improve street lighting.

The Institute completed a large-scale evaluation of improved street lighting in Kansas City, Missouri. The data confirm the public's intuition about street lighting and its relationship to street crime, particularly robbery and assault. The Kansas City study compared the number of nighttime street robberies and assaults in test sites for a one-year period before and after street lighting was improved. In the test sites robberies and assaults decreased by 48 percent, while a decline of only 7 percent was registered in control sites. The results for the test sites are particularly impressive because robberies and assaults in those sections of Kansas City had jumped 36 percent in the two years prior to the study.

The study also investigated the relationship between lighting improvements and crime displacement to other sections of the city. According to the data, a small percentage of the robberies appeared to shift to sections where no lighting improvements

NEW DIRECTIONS IN CRIMINAL JUSTICE RESEARCH

had been made. While further analysis of the problem is required, the study recommended that street lighting improvements be made in large areas, rather than in a three- or four-block section.

The findings of the study make it clear that street lighting has a significant effect on certain types of street crime. The Institute plans to emphasize lighting as an important technique in all future environmental design programs. At the same time, however, we will continue to study the problem of crime displacement resulting from improved lighting.

The Institute plans to distribute the Kansas City findings to communities throughout the country. By providing sound data on the benefits and disadvantages of street lighting improvements, community leaders can plan more effectively, including provisions for dealing with possible crime spillover in other areas.

The Kansas City study is particularly relevant now, when we are searching for ways to conserve energy. Some communities may have considered cutting back on street lighting in an effort to reduce energy consumption. In view of what we now know about the deterrent effect of street lighting, the emphasis should be on finding more efficient lights. The National Institute has recommended that law enforcement and municipal officials consider alternative lighting—such as mercury vapor or high pressure sodium vapor lights—which use far less wattage than incandescent lights to achieve the same illumination.

We have touched upon only a few of the possibilities for reducing crime and rebuilding public confidence in criminal justice. This is necessarily a long-term process which requires a continuing commitment to develop effective, workable programs. While we grapple with these complexities, however, we can begin immediately to heighten our sensitivity to the needs of the "clients" of the system. We know something about how to help them. We ought to start doing it.